M000169470

THE BEDFORD SERIES IN HISTORY AND CULTURE

American Working Women
in World War II

A Brief History with Documents

THE BEDFORD SERIES IN HISTORY AND CULTURE

American Working Women in World War II

A Brief History with Documents

Lynn Dumenil

Occidental College

bedford/st.martin's
Macmillan Learning

Boston | New York

For Bedford/St. Martin's

Vice President, Editorial, Macmillan Learning Humanities: Leasa Burton
Senior Program Director for History: Michael Rosenberg
Senior Executive Program Manager for History: William J. Lombardo
History Marketing Manager: Melissa Rodriguez
Senior Developmental Editor: Heidi L. Hood
Senior Content Project Manager: Lidia MacDonald-Carr
Senior Workflow Project Manager: Jennifer Wetzel
Production Coordinator: Brianna Lester
Executive Media Project Manager: Michelle Camisa
Senior Manager of Publishing Services: Andrea Cava
Project Management: Lumina Datamatics, Inc.
Composition: Lumina Datamatics, Inc.
Director of Rights and Permissions: Hilary Newman
Text Permission Researcher: Mark Schaefer, Lumina Datamatics, Inc.
Permissions Associate: Michael McCarty
Director of Design, Content Management: Diana Blume
Cover Design: William Boardman
Cover Image: Photo by Alfred T. Palmer, Library of Congress, Prints & Photographs
   Division, Reproduction number LC-DIG-fsac-1a35287 (digital file from original
   transparency) LC-USW361-142 (color film copy slide)
Printing and Binding: LSC Communications

Manufactured in the United States of America.

1   2   3   4   5   6   24   23   22   21   20   19

For information, write: Bedford/St. Martin's, 75 Arlington Street, Boston, MA 02116

ISBN 978-1-319-15955-9

Acknowledgments

*Text acknowledgments and copyrights appear at the back of the book on pages 176–78, which
constitute an extension of the copyright page. Art acknowledgments and copyrights appear on
the same page as the art selections they cover.*

To

Libby Sayre and Karen MacLeod

dear friends and labor women *extraordinaire*

Foreword

The Bedford Series in History and Culture is designed so that readers can study the past as historians do.

The historian's first task is finding the evidence. Documents, letters, memoirs, interviews, pictures, movies, novels, or poems can provide facts and clues. Then the historian questions and compares the sources. There is more to do than in a courtroom, for hearsay evidence is welcome, and the historian is usually looking for answers beyond act and motive. Different views of an event may be as important as a single verdict. How a story is told may yield as much information as what it says.

Along the way the historian seeks help from other historians and perhaps from specialists in other disciplines. Finally, it is time to write, to decide on an interpretation and how to arrange the evidence for readers.

Each book in this series contains an important historical document or group of documents, each document a witness from the past and open to interpretation in different ways. The documents are combined with some element of historical narrative — an introduction or a biographical essay, for example — that provides students with an analysis of the primary source material and important background information about the world in which it was produced.

Each book in the series focuses on a specific topic within a specific historical period. Each provides a basis for lively thought and discussion about several aspects of the topic and the historian's role. Each is short enough (and inexpensive enough) to be a reasonable one-week assignment in a college course. Whether as classroom or personal reading, each book in the series provides firsthand experience of the challenge — and fun — of discovering, recreating, and interpreting the past.

Lynn Hunt
David W. Blight
Bonnie G. Smith

Preface

In decades of teaching U.S. Women's history and "war and society" courses, I've learned that students are drawn to the idea of World War II's "Rosie the Riveter"—the defense worker who not only helped win the war, but as a proto-feminist also broke through barriers that had limited women's job opportunities. The source of these notions is undoubtedly the ubiquitous "We Can Do It" image that has become a powerful feminist icon. While this image is a fascinating one, it masks the diversity of women war workers and the larger historical context of their experiences and their lasting impact. This book sets out to widen students' understanding of women's participation in the war while providing a lens through which to examine the history of women, gender, sexuality, labor, race, and ethnicity during this period, as well as the ways in which it may have contributed toward the civil rights movement of the 1950s and the feminist movement of the 1960s. Through a contextual introductory essay and a rich set of primary sources, students have ample material through which to examine this episode in U.S. history.

This book explores a number of questions about the women who worked in the defense industry or enrolled in the military during the war. How diverse were the real women workers of World War II, and what were their experiences? To what extent did they challenge the sex-segregated labor market that had limited women's opportunities? And, what, if anything, was the long-term result of women's dramatic incursion into wartime jobs? While this book's focus is primarily on the war's impact on women, the importance of women to the war effort underscores a key aspect of modern warfare—the essential role of civilians.

The introductory essay in Part One draws on a wealth of scholarship on women and labor and women and war. It sets the context for the war years by offering a brief history of working women in the early twentieth century, paying particular attention to the ways in which women's employment options were profoundly shaped by their gender, race, and ethnicity. The introduction then explores women's wartime experiences and emphasizes the diversity of working women in terms of race, class, ethnicity, age, marital status, and the jobs they tackled. It covers the efforts of African American women to fight job discrimination and the role of women leaders in labor unions in the struggle against sex discrimination. The introduction also addresses the problem of the "second shift"—the labor women performed at home after they returned from their paid jobs—a topic that continues to be a vital issue for working wives and mothers today. In addition, it analyzes the experience of military women by viewing them as engaged in paid labor for the defense effort.

The introduction also explores the long-term impact of the "Rosies" of World War II in the patterns of women's labor and activism. During the war, labor shortages offered all women opportunities for better work and wages, gains that continued to some extent in the postwar years. Despite cultural norms like the feminine mystique that relegated women to the home, women's participation in waged labor steadily increased in the postwar years. Older and married women, including mothers, were more likely to be employed than they had been in the past as well. African American women workers who had protested job discrimination during the war also formed part of the emerging civil rights movement of the 1950s. In addition, women labor activists who had called for creating a work environment adapted to women workers persisted in the postwar years and were part of the coalition of women who founded the feminist organization National Organization for Women in 1966 and played key roles in building post-1960s feminism.

The documents presented in Part Two are varied and engaging. While there are other valuable resources that explore American women and World War II, none provide such a rich collection of materials drawn from oral histories, letters, popular magazines, newspaper accounts, union records, photographs, and government documents. Nor do other works address in such depth the range of women workers—examples of women represented include an African American army officer and a poor African American migrant from the South, a Lakota welder from South Dakota and a Mexican American aircraft worker from Los Angeles, a union organizer and a lesbian in the Women's Army Corps. Besides illustrating the experiences of these working women, the documents allow students to explore government agencies' response to working women as well unions' efforts to organize them and address such issues as childcare and maternity leave. The documents are presented in six chapters and cover the government's campaign to recruit "womanpower"; women defense industry workers; activists in the United Auto Workers and the United Electrical, Radio and Machine Workers unions; the second shift of women's home responsibilities; the experiences of women in the military; and the expectations about women's roles after the end of the war. Each chapter begins with a set of questions for students to consider as they read.

The book's Appendixes contain additional tools to help students get the most form the book. These include a Chronology of American working women in the World War II era, Questions for Consideration, which ask students to consider questions across documents, and a Selected Bibliography of key works to jump-start further research.

ACKNOWLEDGMENTS

My quest for documents for this book was greatly facilitated by librarians and archivists at the National Archives, College Park and Chicago; the Bentley Historical Library, University of Michigan; the VOCES Project at the University of Texas; the Oregon Historical Society; and the Museum of History and Industry, Seattle. Occidental College librarians have been unfailingly helpful; thanks to Carol Siu, John De La Fontaine, and Dale Steiber. Georgia Shaw of Shaw Research and Sally Edelstein also assisted with specific documents.

I'm fortunate, too, in the assistance of the staff at Bedford/ St. Martin's and Macmillan Learning. Thanks to William Lombardo for signing the book and to Heidi L. Hood for her remarkable patience and superb editing. The production work was adeptly managed by Lidia MacDonald-Carr.

A number of instructors provided useful feedback on the first draft manuscript, which informed and strengthened the final work. I appreciate the insights of Mary Kathryn Barbier, Mississippi State University; Dorothea Browder, Western Kentucky University; Angela Elder, Converse College; Keona K. Ervin, University of Missouri; Nicole Jackson, Bowling Green State University; Amy Rutenberg, Iowa State University; Rebecca Sharpless, Texas Christian University; Sarah Sullivan, McHenry County College; and Charles Westmoreland, Delta State University.

I am also extremely grateful for the timely advice from other scholars, including Valerie Matsumoto, Leisa Meyer, Brigid O'Farrell, Vicki Ruiz, Katherine Turk, and Xiaojian Zhao. Elizabeth Escobedo very kindly shared some documents with me on Mexican American women, and Ruth Milkman generously sent me a slew of archival material on union women. My long-time writing buddy, Daniel Horowitz, read an early draft of the introduction, offering his usual insightful suggestions. Sharla Fett read the entire manuscript with a keen eye. As always, my husband and fellow historian, Norman S. Cohen, offered substantial help in improving the manuscript and patiently offering a sounding board over the course of the project.

Lynn Dumenil

Contents

PART ONE

Introduction:
The Women behind the Men
behind the Gun: Working
Women in World War II

Naomi Parker Fraley, the working woman who served as the model for a World War II–era poster of "Rosie the Riveter," died in January 2018. Her death, as well as the complicated story of verifying her identity, made the front page of the *New York Times*. The contemporary interest conveys just how pervasive this iconic image has become, which is all the more surprising because in the 1940s it had a limited audience. During the war, graphic artist J. Howard Miller's poster was displayed within the Westinghouse Electric and Manufacturing Company's factory for a period of only two weeks. Miller's Rosie is white and conventionally feminine despite her strong, flexed muscles. She's carefully made up, and sports remarkably long eyelashes and manicured nails. She wears a polka-dot bandana and work clothes as she tells the viewer, "We Can Do It!" A more widely disseminated image during the war was a second "Rosie," who was created by artist Norman Rockwell and appeared on the cover of posters as well as the popular magazine the *Saturday Evening Post*. Rockwell's Rosie (a name he used, which Miller did not) was also white and wore makeup, but she was heavily muscled and had a powerful looking rivet gun resting on her knee.

Miller's Rosie the Riveter gained fame in the mid-1980s when she was rediscovered by feminists who adopted her as an icon for their movement. Her pervasive appearance on a range of commercial products, from coffee mugs to lunch boxes, enhanced her popularity. Today she continues to

Figure 1. *Rosie the Riveter*

Graphic artist J. Howard Miller created what is now usually called the "We Can Do It" poster for the Westinghouse Electric and Manufacturing Company in 1942 as part of a larger project to boost worker morale at the plant. Naomi Fraley Parker, who worked as an aircraft assembler at the Naval Air Station in Alameda, California, served as Miller's model. Although the poster was displayed only briefly at Westinghouse, the poster of "Rosie the Riveter" became a popular feminist icon in the 1980s and is now one of the most requested images from the National Archives.

National Archives at College Park [535413]

serve as an evocative symbol for feminism. In the 2016 presidential election, campaign buttons for Hillary Clinton imposed her face on the image, and posters of Rosie were omnipresent at the historic woman's march protesting Donald Trump's inauguration in January 2017.

The original image was primarily intended to promote team spirit among Westinghouse workers. But as scholars James J. Kimble and Lester C. Olson note, "Modern audiences . . . reconstruct her as a sort of wartime Everywoman, casting her as a famous representative of women's power on the homefront."[1] Rosie has helped to create a stereotypical view of wartime working women crashing through the barriers that limited women's economic opportunities. She appeals not only because she can be interpreted as exemplifying the way in which women broke through the male-dominated defense industry, but also because she demonstrates her patriotism and by extension her claim to political rights. The iconic Rosie is thus a fitting start to this volume on working women in World War II.

This book focuses on a central set of questions that relate to the image. Who were the American working women of World War II, and how much more diverse were these working women than the Rosie image suggests? How did the work experience of women in the military differ from those with civilian jobs? To what extent did women war workers challenge the sex-segregated labor market that had historically limited women's opportunities? Did women's dramatic incursion into wartime jobs challenge assumptions about women's proper roles in the family and about female sexuality? What do working women's experiences reveal about race relations and an emerging civil rights movement? How did the war facilitate women's activism in labor unions? Beyond economic opportunities, did the war promote women's social and political power? And finally, how does women's war work help us to understand a key aspect of modern warfare — the essential roles of civilians? Through a range of documents — oral histories, newspapers, magazines, photographs, advertisements, and government documents — this book reveals the vital role of American women in mobilizing for World War II and constructs a complex sense of the women who performed this work.

WORKING WOMEN IN THE EARLY TWENTIETH CENTURY

To understand World War II women's work experience, we need first to examine women and work before the war. By the late nineteenth century the labor demands of the nation's rapid industrialization after the Civil War had propelled a significant number of American women into the labor force. In 1890, 18.2 percent of them worked for wages; by 1910, the number had grown to 24.8 percent. This labor market was divided by sex, race, and ethnicity with female laborers clustered in positions understood to be "women's" jobs. In factories, women performed less skilled tasks. In white-collar occupations they found work in the feminized professions of teaching and nursing and as office workers, sales clerks, and telephone operators. These so-called women's jobs were characterized by lower status and lower wages. This benefited employers in search of low-cost workers and assured male workers that they would dominate better-paid and more highly skilled jobs. The notion of "women's" jobs also reinforced the notion that women were secondary wage earners, whose real work was in the home. As one historian has explained, sex-segregated labor "minimized the cultural disjuncture between the need for labor and the cultural expectations of woman's domestic role."[2]

Women's labor was also characterized by racial and ethnic segmentation in the early twentieth century. White native-born women dominated the feminized professions as well as office work. European immigrant daughters filled positions in textiles, garment, and shoe factories, where they met with harsh conditions and poor wages. Domestic and personal service was performed primarily by foreign-born and black women. Women of color, especially African Americans but also Asian and Mexican Americans, made up much of the female agricultural labor force. Although there were exceptions, such as opportunities in tobacco plants, African Americans, who still lived primarily in the South, were denied industrial jobs. In 1910 over 90 percent of African American women were in farm labor or domestic service. A tiny proportion found work as teachers, social workers, and nurses, but here, too, they met with much discrimination. Whatever their race, ethnicity, or marital status, as the century began, all working women were disadvantaged by an inherently unequal labor market.[3]

Ironically, social reforms of the Progressive Era (ca. 1890–1914), designed to help poor working women, especially in urban factories, tended to reinforce this inequality. Although a few states enacted minimum wage laws, a handful of others passed laws to restrict the hours women might work and to prohibit night work completely. The assumption was that all working women were potential mothers whose reproductive functions could be damaged by harsh working conditions. While these laws may have served women well by protecting them from exploitation, many historians argue that they also emphasized that women were inherently vulnerable, underlining the assumption of women's inequality as workers.[4]

When the United States entered World War I in April 1917, the rigidity of sex-segregated labor temporarily eroded. With men drafted into the army and European immigration cut off by the conflict, labor scarcity forced employers to hire women for what were considered "men's" jobs. And, moreover, racial segmentation broke down. The war helped create the Great Migration of an estimated 500,000 African American men and women from the South to the North. "Pushed" by discrimination, disenfranchisement, and violence in the South, they were "pulled" by the lure of better jobs and the hope for more freedom in cities like Chicago, Detroit, and New York. For the first time, black women, who had been almost exclusively employed in domestic and agricultural labor, found their way into factory work, although usually in the dirtiest and most dangerous jobs and only for a brief period of wartime mobilization.

Most of the wartime women workers, both white and black, had some previous paid employment. Perhaps as few as 5 percent had not worked before. War work meant that working-class women had access to more desirable and better paid jobs. While they continued to work in positions usually associated with women, such as textiles, laundries, food processing, and clerical work, significant numbers filled jobs traditionally held by men. Uniformed women served as streetcar conductors and elevator operators. They worked for the railroads and performed heavy physical labor. And they entered industries largely closed to them previously: steel, iron, chemicals, and the metal trades, most of which were associated with defense work. Women working in government arsenals garnered much publicity because of the direct connection to military needs, as did the small numbers of women who served in the military, mostly in clerical capacities on the home front.

The phenomenon of women crossing workplace boundaries by taking jobs typically held by men created much public interest. Magazines and newspapers described what they interpreted as a major transformation in the workforce. And they illustrated this trend with photographs and drawings of women at work, often wearing pants or overalls, a dramatic break with respectable female attire. Yet despite the excitement, women who crossed these boundaries experienced much discrimination. Nurses in the U.S. Army were denied military rank, which meant they were not allowed to be officers. They viewed this as an insult that limited their authority in dealing with patients and with male military personnel. At home, defense industries with federal contracts were supposed to adhere to the principle of "equal pay for equal work," a requirement that came in part as a result of unions insisting that women laborers should not undercut male wages by working for less money. Yet even when they performed the same work as men, their labor was usually categorized in such a way that equal pay was rarely achieved. For example, although men and women might be performing the same tasks, women's classification might be termed as "light" and men's as "skilled." In addition, women often experienced hostility on the part of employers and male coworkers. Thus, while Americans marveled at the way in which women took on men's work during World War I, conventional notions concerning women's place in the workforce persisted.

This became more evident at war's end as women lost most of the access to the higher paid jobs they'd had during the war. Women's opportunities were also unevenly divided among women after the war. With some exceptions, most African American women failed to keep their industrial jobs and found themselves back in domestic or farm work. However, after the war white women increased their participation in clerical work, where they clustered in positions deemed more suitable for women. In 1910, they constituted 37.4 percent of office workers. By 1920, that figure was 49.6 percent and, moreover, the clerical work represented the largest sector of jobs for women, comprising 25.6 percent of those who were employed. Women's participation in professions, although mostly feminized ones like teaching and social work, also increased in the same period (from 9.1 to 11.9 percent).[5]

Between the First and Second World Wars, a number of developments stand out in the history of American women's labor. In the 1920s, women's rights activists divided sharply over approaches to improving women's position in the workplace. Self-described feminists in the National Woman's Party (formerly a suffrage organization) called for an Equal Rights Amendment (ERA). Introduced in Congress in 1923, the ERA called simply for equal rights for men and women, with the intention that the amendment would implement equal rights in all aspects of public life, not just in employment. Pitted against them were women social reformers, including those associated with the newly created League of Women Voters and the federal Women's Bureau in the U.S. Department of Labor (established just as World War I was ending). They insisted that such a "blanket" amendment would invalidate the protective labor legislation for women that many states had enacted. Although women in the latter group endorsed the concept of equal legal rights for women, they continued to view women workers as vulnerable, especially because of their child-bearing potential, and thus in need of protection. The division over the ERA ran deep and would continue to divide women activists until the 1970s, when "second wave" feminists embraced the ERA, although again without success.

Sex-segregated labor patterns persisted in the interwar period. Between 1920 and 1940, the percentage of working women increased only slightly (23.9 percent in 1920 and 25.4 percent in 1940), but married women's participation grew more noticeably, with married women making up 23 percent of the female workforce in 1920 and 35 percent of this workforce in 1940. Many observers in the 1920s expressed concern with the growing trend of wives in the workplace. As one marriage expert put it, "When the woman herself earns and her maintenance is not entirely at the mercy of her husband's will, diminishing masculine authority necessarily follows."[6]

The onset of the Great Depression in 1929 generated even more anxiety about working wives. With widespread economic collapse, unemployment reached a high in 1933 of approximately one-fourth of the entire workforce. The crisis was invariably described as one of the "forgotten man," with an emphasis not merely on the economic hardship of unemployment but also the psychological damage to men unable to fill their breadwinner role. Public opinion polls revealed strong resentment of married women who worked. Besides hostile public commentary about wives working, many states banned them from government jobs, and the Federal Emergency Act of 1932 required that if employees were to be fired, families with more than one government employee would be targeted first. Supervisors routinely used this law to justify letting married women go. At the same time, thousands of school districts barred the employment of married women.

Despite these obstacles, married women, often sole supports of their families, increased their participation in paid employment. Ironically, women workers in general may have benefited from the pattern of sex segregation in the labor force. Although in the first years of the Depression, women lost jobs more rapidly than men, by 1933, their conditions improved. Sectors of the economy where women predominated—light industry—recovered more quickly than heavy manufacturing, where men dominated the workforce. The New Deal, President Franklin D. Roosevelt's program to stimulate recovery and provide assistance to unemployed and impoverished Americans, as well as state agencies expanded government bureaucracies. Their efforts to combat the problems of the Depression led to increased demand for clerical workers and human resource specialists, which benefited women. Women's wages continued to be low, especially compared to men's, and women continued to be viewed as secondary or marginal wage earners, regardless of their role in family financial support. But, nonetheless, they persisted in the workforce.[7]

ROSIE THE RIVETER AND THE PROPAGANDA CAMPAIGN

World War II ended the devastating Great Depression and the crisis of unemployment. The European war, which began in 1939, created markets for American goods, which in turn stimulated the economy, as did the beginning of defense mobilization at home. Between 1939 and the end of the war in 1945, the American economy recovered from the Depression and then boomed. As Americans went back to work, it was men who first found employment. Most U.S. firms resisted converting their plants to defense production, and it was not until after the bombing of Pearl Harbor (December 7, 1941) and the American entrance into the war that mobilization began in earnest. Even then, employers had little interest in recruiting and training women for what often was called "the arsenal of democracy." Government planners, however, were convinced that a labor crisis was inevitable and that the demands of modern warfare could be resolved only by attracting white housewives or middle-class daughters to defense jobs. It was assumed that these women, unlike poor or ethnic and racial-minority women, would not ordinarily be interested in paid labor, especially industrial labor.

That contemporary Americans have at least a vague notion of women defense workers in World War II is due largely to the extraordinary outpouring of information, stories, and images engineered during the war by U.S. government propaganda agencies, most notably the Office of War Information (OWI), which worked closely with the War Manpower Commission (WMC). Also important was the War Advertising Council, a private agency that worked closely with the OWI and encouraged companies to run public service advertisements. In late 1942, these agencies began a massive publicity "womanpower" campaign aimed at white married women and mothers without young children, to encourage them to seek jobs related to defense and to join the military. The government also urged women to seek out clerical and other more typical women's work at a time when all sectors of the war economy needed workers. Newspapers, magazines, advertisements, film, and radio all enthusiastically echoed the WMC's call for patriotic women to join the workforce (Documents 1–7).

Whether describing a riveter, an army officer, or a typist, the Office of War Information and the War Manpower Commission constructed a consistent vision of working women in wartime. The campaign portrayed them as competent, resourceful, and efficient, and generally as white. But despite their accomplishments, the propaganda made it clear that their work did not endanger their femininity or make them "mannish," a euphemism used to describe lesbians. In encouraging women to work, the government seemingly challenged conventional notions of women's proper place, yet the womanpower campaign carefully promoted messages to the contrary. The campaign implied that these women worked not primarily for goals of financial reward or independence, but rather out of patriotic willingness to serve the nation in time of war. By serving, they would earn the respect of their communities, especially their husbands and the men with whom they worked. That women were taking the place of men at the front — and thus only temporarily in the workplace — further reinforced the argument that war work did not permanently threaten conventional expectations about women's roles.[8]

Other popular culture images downplayed the potential threat that "Rosie" posed to the gender order. Idealized housewives and mothers remained more evident in print media and movies than did working women. Office of War Information propaganda glamorized housewives' role in the war, as they maintained the home front and supported the war effort through food conservation and war bond purchases (Document 6). And, new to the war were the ubiquitous "pin-up" girls, photographs of movie stars in bathing suits with lots of "cheesecake," the term for women's exposed flesh. Servicemen adorned their lockers and barracks and even airplanes with pictures of women like the actress Betty Grable, who in many ways personified the innocent girl next door — only with million-dollar legs. More obviously sexy was the sultry Rita Hayworth, another major movie star of the period. At the same time, young women were coached by movie magazines on how to create their own image as a pin-up girl to send to their boyfriends and husbands. The sexualized woman they left behind became one of the symbols of what men were fighting for — a home adorned with a lovely woman. She was sexy, but that sexuality was contained and domesticated by her role as wife and mother. The glorification of housewives and pin-ups made it clear that mainstream popular culture for the most part reaffirmed women's place in the home, particularly the patriotic home.[9]

A few voices, however, did offer a different perspective on women and work in wartime. National Woman's Party feminists persisted in their campaign for the ERA and emphasized the need for equal pay. Their audience was primarily a small group of elite professional women, whose concerns were far from women working in defense industries and other manual labor jobs. The Women's Bureau (a federal agency established in 1920) continued to be alert to issues of working women's health and safety. The bureau had little influence with agencies like the War Manpower Commission, which did not have any women on its staff but included a woman's advisory committee whose input was largely ignored. Nonetheless, Women's Bureau agents visited major plants to encourage good working conditions and equal pay. They also conducted a series of surveys and reports on women defense workers, filled with statistics on wages, hours, and former employment patterns. The media published some extracts from these reports, which provided a far more realistic sense of actual working women than government propaganda (Document 48). But in the absence of a mass movement for women's rights, there was little attention given to a more women-centered evaluation of the meaning of women's war work.[10]

THE WOMEN WAR WORKERS OF WORLD WAR II

At first glance, the wartime push to recruit women who might otherwise not have sought employment succeeded. Nineteen million women worked during World War II, and six million of them were classified as "new" workers. Yet who were these women workers? Many, like Gene Dickson, may well have been the women the War Manpower Commission targeted. As Dickson explained, "On December 7 last I gave my house a fine cleaning, washed up the dinner dishes and went to work in an airplane factory, night shift, along with thousands of other housewives like myself."[11] But a careful look at the statistics suggests a more complicated profile for World War II women workers. In 1940, an estimated three million women were unemployed and actively looking for work. Moreover, many of the women who were characterized as "new" had paid employment earlier in their lives. The number of workers genuinely new to paid labor was probably closer to 3.5 million, and this number was in keeping with the persistent increase in women working over the course of the twentieth century. In other words, the war offered women opportunities for employment, but the war and the recruitment campaign do not in themselves explain the growth in women's participation in the workforce. Women may have worked out of patriotic goals, but they also served their own agendas of financial need and personal satisfaction.[12]

Moreover, the war may well have stimulated a key shift in women's employment patterns. For the first time in American history, there were more married women than single women in the workforce. In 1944, married women constituted 44 percent of the female workforce, while single women accounted for 42.7 percent, and the figure for widows or divorcées was 13.0 percent.[13] Some of these married women were the wives of servicemen away from home who supplemented the family income in the face of low wages for men in the military (Documents 13 and 30). This cohort fits best the WMC's vision of female war workers. But more than 60 percent of new laborers were women over thirty-five years old, suggesting what would become increasingly common: married women were joining or returning to the workforce after their children started school. While these women had their own goals of contributing to family resources, the propaganda that stressed housewives' patriotic duty made it more acceptable for married women to work than it had during the decade of the Great Depression when hostility to working wives was so evident.

The statistics of women working in World War II merit further unpacking. Women of color may well have experienced the most significant improvement in their work lives. As was the case with the First World War, World War II stimulated a large migration of black men and women. Within the South, a million moved to the cities. Another 1.5 million left the South and flocked to the urban North and Midwest, as well as the West Coast, where airplane factories and shipbuilding flourished (Document 8). Most defense industries were slow to hire black women and when they did they were most likely to place them in unskilled and unpleasant work, such as positions in foundries and outdoor labor gangs. At best, black men and women combined constituted about 6 percent of jobs in the aircraft industry when they constituted close to 10 percent of the nation's population. By contrast white women held down 40 percent of these jobs. Beyond defense work, black women also found clerical jobs, especially working for government agencies, but they still comprised only 1.6 percent of all female clerical workers. But perhaps the most significant entry into better jobs came when white women left less desirable work in factories, thus freeing up positions for African Americans in such industries as textiles and food processing.[14]

A similar process took place for other women of color. Many Chinese, Filipina, and Mexican American women had access to factory work previously denied them and met with less discrimination than black women did in defense industry jobs (Documents 10, 11, 14, and 15). In the Midwest, a Mexican American woman reported that employers "stopped asking for proof of legalization because they needed all the workers they could find for the war effort."[15] And in Los Angeles, aircraft companies actively recruited ethnic minority women. As garment industry workers, Mexican American women made $8–$10 a week.

In defense work, as riveters, punch press operators, and welders, their wages often came to $60 a week. Even women in the notoriously low-paid and low-status food processing industry benefited from war conditions. Food processing became vital to the war effort, and in California the United Cannery, Agricultural, Packing, and Allied Workers Union negotiated contracts with better wages and conditions.[16] Beyond the improved income that defense workers received, wartime jobs helped to raise expectations. Rose Echeverría, a Los Angeles aircraft worker put it this way: "We felt that if we worked hard and that if we proved ourselves, we, too, could become doctors and lawyers and professional people." The war, according to historian Elizabeth R. Escobedo, had "contributed to a softening of racial boundaries."[17]

Native American women, too, found new work available to them in defense industries. In 1941 and 1942, the government designated six Indian Service boarding schools for defense training. In its first years of operation, for example, the Oklahoma Chilocco School trained 175 students, 85 percent of whom found employment. Although both young men and women received instruction, women initially were not taught the most highly skilled and highly paid work but instead took home economics or business courses. As the demand for women's labor increased, they learned welding and machine shop skills (in the second year, the school enrolled twenty-four women and three men) and found jobs in the aircraft industry, in shipbuilding, and in ordnance plants (Document 12).[18]

A notable exception to these opportunities in defense work was the experience of Japanese American women. In the West, the federal government bowed to nativist and racist pressure to incarcerate in relocation camps people of Japanese descent, citizen and noncitizen alike. Located in desolate places, these camps were enclosed by barbed wire and guarded by armed soldiers. The accommodations were primitive. Families had little privacy and limited freedom. Uprooted from their homes and subjected to the regimentation of camp life, both immigrant women (Issei) and their American-born daughters (Nisei) found their lives profoundly disrupted. In some cases, they volunteered to work in agriculture, assisting with the sugar beet harvest in states like Idaho or plucking turkeys in Utah. The work was arduous, but many concluded, as one woman put it, "it is worth the freedom we are allowed."[19] The camps also employed the internees in administrative work, and Nisei women used their English skills and education to good effect. Earning the same wages as men, camp jobs may well have fostered a sense of independence in these young women who had been tightly bound in a largely patriarchal culture. In 1942, when the government began to allow Nisei to leave the camps, some Nisei women joined the military, while others migrated to the Midwest and East Coast, where they found a variety of jobs (Documents 41 and 51). As was the case with other women of color, the war ultimately opened up positions in clerical and industrial work.

The types of work women took on during the war were as diverse as the women themselves. As eager as the War Manpower Commission was to encourage women to enlist in military service or to enter into defense work, it also worried about labor shortages in the mainstream economy. Thus, its propaganda campaign reminded women that those "who fill the shoes of any men who have left those occupations which are necessary to the life and well being of the civilian population are doing *war work* just as surely as if they donned military uniform of factory overalls."[20]

One form of such work that seemingly challenged gender norms for white women was farm labor. While women of color often worked as farm laborers, white women were less likely to labor in the fields as hired hands. The war changed this at least temporarily. Both the military and the lure of high-paying factory jobs seriously depleted the supply of farm laborers (by the end of the war over six million men had left agricultural work). White farm wives took up some of the slack, adding fieldwork to their household responsibilities. Foreign workers were recruited, most notably from Mexico through the Bracero program, which offered contracts to men that were supposed to guarantee them fair wages and conditions, a guarantee not always met. Mexican women sometimes accompanied their menfolk, illegally, providing household support and often going into the fields. Many Japanese Americans were released temporarily from internment camps to work in local agriculture, and this included many women. Black, Mexican, and Filipina women, too, continued their farm labor, although many found better work in defense industries.

None of this labor, however, was sufficient, and early in the war many called for a Women's Land Army agricultural program to meet farm labor needs, noting the precedent set in World War I and the successful British Land Army in World War II. In April 1943, the federal government finally created the Women's Land Army (WLA). Statistics are hard to come by, but historians estimate that between 1943 and 1945, 1.5 million nonfarm women, many of them teachers and students, enrolled. Farm women, too, became part of the program, especially in the Midwest, where large-scale farming required operating expensive equipment like tractors, jobs farmers were unwilling to entrust to unknown city women. By 1944 forty-four states had WLA training programs for city and farm women. WLA work varied. Women might harvest fruit and vegetables, milk cows, drive tractors and trucks, or wield hoes and shovels. WLA women were roundly praised for their patriotic labor. The temporary nature of WLA work—some women worked for just a few weeks, for example—diffused concern about women taking on male jobs.

Beyond farm work, many women were taking on other nonindustrial jobs formerly viewed as men's. Thus the Office of War Information reported that almost sixty women were driving taxicabs in Philadelphia and that in Salt Lake City service stations employed women who pumped gas and repaired tires. In Buffalo, New York, "every drygoods store, news stand, restaurant, grocery store and butcher shop has women behind the counters." The same report noted, however, that in areas where large defense plants operated, like Norfolk, Virginia, "[b]ig war wages in the Navy Yard and other war plants is the reason women are leaving civilian service jobs."[21]

Although women clearly sought out a range of opportunities in the civilian economy, the lure of defense work was compelling. Not only were the wages significantly better, but these jobs had the allure of high-profile patriotic service. Because it was in defense work in which women most profoundly seemed to challenge gender expectations and the sex-segregated labor market, we focus here primarily on women in wartime industries.

ROSIE AND HER SISTERS: DEFENSE INDUSTRY JOBS

Even in defense factories, where the bulk of women's war work contributions took place, not all women were "Rosies" performing manual labor. A significant portion of women in the defense sector were white-collar workers. For the period 1940–1944, women's participation in manufacturing rose significantly (20.2 to 29.9 percent), but clerical work sustained almost as much growth (21.3 to 26.6 percent).[22] Many office workers held down jobs in the war-expanded government bureaucracy. As early as 1942, an estimated 60 percent of all federal employees were women. In the first year of the war alone, 40,000 stenographers and typists joined the government workforce in Washington, D.C. Office workers also found jobs in defense manufacturing as typists, bookkeepers, and technicians (Documents 9, 10, and 13). In most cases, these companies paid white-collar employees well, compared to the civilian sectors. Such work had a strong appeal, especially to middle-class women. It was cleaner than factory work, and it did not require they wear laborers' clothes, hair coverings, and the like. Moreover, women could expect that clerical work, like other feminized labor, might prove more stable in the long run.

Compared to office workers, professional women enjoyed fewer new opportunities in industry in the war era. Women's rights reformers like Virginia Gildersleeve, Dean at Barnard College, did succeed in getting some universities to open doors or improve quotas for women students in sciences and technology. Women apparently seized these opportunities. Between 1940 and 1945, 181 women received undergraduate degrees in engineering, representing an increase of 75 percent. But the government and private corporations preferred short-term training to provide woman "brainpower" in defense work. The Engineering, Science, and Management War Training program, funded by the government for both male and female students in defense-related academic subjects like engineering and chemistry, trained 282,000 women during the war.[23] And a number of corporations also funded technical training specific to their industries.

Although these programs offered women new opportunities, they did not "prepare women as full-fledged members of the scientific community for professional life."[24] These women were considered "aides" or junior engineers as both the government and corporations viewed them as temporary solutions. General Electric's Turbine Department, for example, explained that it hired female math majors with the specific goal of relieving male "engineers of as much calculating work as possible, and thus permit them to concentrate on the more involved problems for which their specialized training has fit them."[25] With these attitudes, it is not surprising that the war created little in the way of permanent inroads for women scientists or engineers.[26]

The most dramatic development in women's work, both in terms of numbers and in public perception, was of course the flood of women into blue-collar defense jobs. Statistics for the aircraft industry capture the novelty: in April 1941, only 143 women were employed in that sector; by October 1943, their numbers had soared to 65,000.[27] Women also built ships; worked in the steel, automobile, and ammunition industries; and expanded their presence in defense-related concerns like meatpacking and railways. As they took on jobs formerly assumed to be exclusively male, they wore masculinized clothing—overalls, denim jeans, or trousers. In the interest of safety, they covered their hair with caps or bandanas and left their jewelry at home.

Despite the boundaries they crossed — in terms of work and dress — there were limits to how much women workers challenged the pervasive sex segregation in the labor market. Women rarely had management jobs in defense industries. Certainly there were women who obtained enough training to take on skilled work like welding and riveting, but women represented only a small percentage of these workers. In most industries, employers streamlined or reorganized processes so that women were assigned to jobs like assembly or inspection. "Rosie the Riveter did a 'man's job,'" one scholar has explained, "but more often than not she worked in a predominantly female department or job classification. The boundaries between women's and men's work shifted their location, but were not eliminated."[28]

The persistence of sex segregation was also reflected in women's wages. Defense work generally paid well. Government contracts stipulated a "cost-plus" provision so that manufacturers were guaranteed a profit regardless of their costs. This, as well as labor scarcity, made employers more amenable to improved wages. As was the case in World War I, both the federal government and unions called for "equal pay" for women doing men's work. There were some forces within unions and government agencies like the Women's Bureau that viewed equal pay in terms of genuine equity for women, but the real engine propelling equal pay was safeguarding male earnings (Document 19).[29] Even though many women did receive equal pay, because employers created "women's" classifications within defense industries, most women's wages were significantly lower than men's. Historian Alice Kessler-Harris estimates that in 1939, women on average earned 62 percent of men's wages, while in the war era that figure dropped to 55 percent. Some of the differential may have been the result of men generally working longer hours than women. A majority of states limited women's working hours, and although manufacturers could request exemptions, most full-time working women probably worked forty-eight hours per week, while men worked fifty-four. But the classification of "women's" jobs also was a significant factor in their lower earnings (Documents 18–20).[30]

Despite the inequity between men's and women's earnings, most female defense industry workers viewed their wages as dramatic improvement. Indeed, high wages were what had propelled them into the factories. "The money was too good to pass up," commented Jean Clark, who had quit high school to work in a shipyard in the Northwest.[31] This was especially true for women who had worked in service jobs. A Women's Bureau survey, for example, estimated that fully 30 percent of waitresses left their jobs for defense work. One woman reported that her wages had been 20 cents an hour, in contrast to the $1.15 she earned at a bomber plant in Willow Run Detroit.[32]

FIGHTING RACE DISCRIMINATION

For all the positive aspects of defense jobs, women nonetheless faced many challenges, none more so than African American women. The scholarly concept of "intersectionality," which posits the way in which racial, sexual, and class identity combine to shape the experiences of women of color, captures the situation of African American working women in World War II well.[33] Usually poor, they found their employment opportunities limited by both race and gender. Historically, the racism of both white employees and employers led to resistance to hiring black women for industrial labor that would have offered them better pay and conditions. This prejudice persisted as war mobilization heated up and most defense corporations initially refused to hire African Americans, a problem that was particularly acute for black women.

But the war eventually brought African Americans some avenues for fighting racial discrimination in war industries. In 1940, after the African American "March on Washington Movement" threatened a massive rally in Washington, D.C., to protest segregation in the military and discrimination in defense industries, President Roosevelt issued Executive Order 8802, which created the Fair Employment Practices Committee (FEPC). Roosevelt ignored the military issue, but did authorize a federal agency charged with addressing discrimination in defense industries and government on the basis of race, color, creed, or national origins. Sex was not an included category. Mexican Americans used the FEPC in small numbers, as did Jewish and other ethnic Americans. African Americans, however, comprised the bulk of complainants (90 percent), and of those women accounted for 30 percent.[34]

The FEPC was only moderately successful in reversing deeply rooted patterns of discrimination. Its power to force companies to hire African Americans and treat them fairly was constrained by limited resources and weak means of enforcement. FEPC efforts were also stymied by the dilemma of needing to keep vital war production in place, when employers were unwilling to address discriminatory practices. And discrimination was widespread. Although African American men certainly met with resistance, black women were invariably "the last hired and first fired." As late as 1943, a survey revealed that only 74 of the 280 production industries canvassed hired black women.[35] African

American women who had received training were refused jobs and if they were hired, usually denied positions their training entitled them to and instead offered jobs as janitorial workers or other low-status positions. White workers' "race strikes" over the hiring of both black men and women in cities such as Baltimore and Detroit made it clear that it was not just employers who discriminated. In many communities, white women refused to work with black women, drawing upon racist notions about cleanliness and immorality (Document 57).[36]

In the face of these obstacles, African American women filed complaints with their local FEPC (Documents 16 and 17). Detailing their skills and training and emphasizing their patriotism, they drew upon the rhetoric of democracy to justify their right to work and their right to fair and respectful treatment.[37] In most regions, especially the South, FEPC committees were slow to respond to black women's cases and often met with intractable resistance, as was the case in Kingsbury, Indiana. There, Todd & Brown, a large munitions factory, not only segregated labor by sex, but by race as well. The company refused to hire more than 10 percent of African Americans of either sex. If a job held by a white woman became available, the company would request that United States Employment Service fill the position with another white woman. It claimed that by maintaining this quota, it demonstrated that they were willing to hire black women and therefore they did not discriminate. The FEPC failed to change the company's policy.

In contrast to the disappointing FEPC results in Kingsbury, the FEPC met with more success in communities that had strong local activists and sympathetic unions. In Detroit, for example, there was a vibrant National Association for the Advancement of Colored People (NAACP) and a branch of the civil rights organization the Urban League. There was also a specially created local committee, the Metropolitan Detroit Council of Fair Employment Practices. While some unions persisted in racist and sexist policies, the dominant union in Detroit, the United Auto Workers, supported efforts to challenge racial discrimination, and Detroit civil rights activists worked with the UAW to improve employment opportunities for African Americans. The UAW's and NAACP's 1942 four-hour demonstration at Ford Motor Company's Willow Run facilities over the failure of the company to hire black women resulted in Ford's decision to hire twenty-seven African American women. In Detroit and elsewhere, unions and the FEPC were also active in quelling hate strikes (Document 27) that centered around hiring black women and the integrated use of bathroom and lunch facilities. In many cases, union officials told white women strikers that they could either work with black women or give up their jobs. By the end of the war, many factories continued to maintain segregated facilities, but some progress had been made in terms of job opportunities; the numbers of African American women employed in the defense industry rose from less than thirty women in June 1942 to 14,000 seventeen months later.[38]

Scholars are divided over the success of the FEPC's efforts on behalf of black men and women. On the one hand, in the case of women, their percentages in defense industries certainly increased in Detroit and many other cities. On the other hand, severe labor shortages rather than FEPC or community pressure may account for much of this growth. Rather than emphasize the FEPC's success, it is more useful to view it as a factor that made World War II a seedbed for the civil rights movement that would emerge in the 1950s. Drawing upon the FEPC, civil rights organizations, and progressive unions, African Americans mobilized to resist discrimination during World War II—a process in which African American women were central.

FIGHTING SEX DISCRIMINATION: UNION WOMEN AND THE U.S. WOMEN'S BUREAU

Just as progressive unions challenged race discrimination during the war, they were also vehicles for offering women some recourse for addressing gender discrimination in defense industries. When the United States began mobilizing for war, male union leaders resisted hiring women for what were viewed as men's jobs. Most male-dominated labor unions were hostile, and many actively protested women's employment in defense industries and determined to bar women from union membership. But as the demand for labor mushroomed and women's presence in defense industries skyrocketed, unions bowed to the inevitable. Women's participation in unions increased dramatically. In 1940, women constituted only 9.4 percent of union members; in 1944, the figure was 21.8 percent. Women's union participation was particularly notable in the UAW, which counted 28 percent women among its one million members—a significant increase over the 10 percent of women in 1939. Even more impressive was women's participation in the notably progressive United Electrical, Radio and Machine Workers of America (UE), with 40 percent women among its 700,000 members, although it should be noted women had been more present in the industry and in the union before World War II than in most other industries and unions, with 15 percent of its members women in early 1942.[39]

Both of these unions were affiliates of the Congress of Industrial Organizations (CIO), established in 1935. Unlike the mostly trade-based American Federation of Labor, the CIO organized entire industries, such as meatpacking, steel, and auto workers to give workers more leverage with corporations. To do so meant that unions needed to include all types of workers—skilled and unskilled, among whom were minority and immigrant workers, and occasionally women. The CIO's commitment to inclusive unions was also shaped by the presence of many Communist organizers in the CIO who sought to convince workers to view themselves as a class and not let other divisions, especially racial ones, impede their ability to achieve leverage in the battle against corporate power. It was not until World War II and the dramatic expansion of women into a variety of mass industries, however, that most CIO unions took much interest in organizing women.

In response to women's encroachment onto male workers' turf, many male union leaders initially focused primarily on minimizing the threat to male wages by insisting upon "equal pay for equal work." While the concept benefited women workers, it was most importantly a means of ensuring that employers not depress wages by exploiting women as cheaper labor. Unions won success for this principle when the National War Labor Board—a federal agency established to mediate between defense industry employers and their workers—decreed in 1942 that "wages rates for women shall be the same as for men where they do work of comparable quantity and quality in comparable operations."[40] While corporations continued to find ways to classify work in such a way as to funnel women into jobs that were lower paid, the principle of equal pay and the subsequent difficulty of determining the nature of women's work descriptions sowed the seeds for a broader questioning of the inherent inequality of most "women's jobs" that would emerge in the decade after the war.

Although many male union leaders sought to contain the threat posed by women's encroachment, the war emergency created new leadership opportunities for women in unions (Documents 18, 20, and 26). The UE and the UAW, for example, created training courses so that women could take the place of male organizers who entered the military. In the UE, UAW, and United Packinghouse Workers of America, women were elected to offices and served as delegates to conventions. The UAW was notable for creating a women's committee, which held a number of conferences during the war years and in 1946 set up a permanent Women's Bureau of its own. And in many unions, especially those in textiles and the food industry, Mexican American and African American women emerged as activists.

In these new leadership roles, union women focused on educating new workers into the value of union membership and loyalty, but they also raised questions about discrimination women faced in the workforce and in the unions themselves. They demanded more rigorous attention to the questions of equal pay and the seniority system (for determining the order of layoffs and rehiring). They also encouraged unions to address so-called women's issues, with childcare and maternity benefits being especially significant. As a rule, most union women did not challenge sex segregation per se; rather they called for upgrading the status and pay of "women's" jobs and facilitating ways for women to meet their dual needs as workers and mothers (Documents 19, 20, 25, and 26).

When the war ended, manufacturers laid off women in huge numbers (see below). Reluctant to take women on in the first place, employers were eager to purge women from the workplace and return to the former system of the male-dominated factory floor. In a number of industries, union women mobilized to protest their firing, especially when men with less seniority were kept on and restored to jobs after initial layoffs (Document 56). Although there were exceptions, most male union leaders failed to support the women, in part because they were anxious about economic uncertainties and the security of men's jobs in the reconversion period. Nonetheless women staged protests and filed grievances. In May 1945, for example, UAW women called a plant-wide meeting for women by issuing a flyer that proclaimed, "LISTEN, BROTHERS! We're Union Members, Too—and We Intend to Stay That Way." Women also persisted in filing complaints with their unions over issues of seniority and pay, though with little success, either because of male workers' indifference or employer resistance.[41]

Little came of their efforts immediately after the war, but within a few years, plants did begin to hire women, although usually in traditionally women's jobs, not the skilled and better paid ones they had had access to during the war. And, their increased numbers also meant a steady increase in union membership. In 1940, only 800,000 women had been in unions. Ten years after the war ended, in 1956, that number was 3.5 million. Between 1940 and 1956, the percentage of union members who were women doubled, to 18 percent.[42] In these years, more unions created separate women's bureaus, which facilitated women's activism. Female union leaders consistently fought for more equal treatment. They lobbied successfully to get their unions to include antidiscrimination language (concerning seniority and marital status, for example) and equal pay provisions in their contracts. Maternity leave was also a crucial demand. Female union leaders also encouraged women to become engaged in politics to support labor-friendly legislation.

During the war and after, union women leaders were assisted in their struggles against discrimination by the U.S. Women's Bureau, which from its inception had worked closely with union activists (Documents 18, 26, and 48). The Bureau had little influence with the War Manpower Commission, but it did try to counter the notion of woman as temporary workers "for the duration." In the postwar years, the Bureau, in concert with union women, would also lobby (unsuccessfully) for a federal Equal Pay Act. Although it hoped to improve women's employment opportunities, the social climate of the immediate postwar years meant that the Women's Bureau tended to encourage women to seek work in fields where they would not compete with men, that is, traditional women's jobs. Perhaps most important, in sponsoring two conferences of union women, one in 1945 and another the following year, it created a forum for "labor feminists," as historian Dorothy Sue Cobble calls them, to articulate their concerns and formulate an agenda. This agenda included an end to discrimination based on sex, race, ethnicity, marital status, and age. These women called for "abolishing wage differentials based on sex rather than job content," fair access to promotion, improved labor standards, and more respect for "woman-employing" occupations. They also emphasized the need for maternity and childcare support.[43]

Both the Women's Bureau and most women labor leaders shared a long-standing hostility to the ERA, and their discussions of the need for protective legislation and policies for women underlined that their focus was not on always treating men and women alike in the workplace (Document 21). Most of these leaders believed that physiological differences, or at least motherhood, did create special needs for some women. "They wanted equality *and* special treatment," one historian has argued, "and they did not think of the two as incompatible. . . . Theirs was a vision of equality that claimed justice on the basis of their humanity, not on the basis of their sameness with men."[44] In the postwar years, however, the emphasis on protective legislation eroded as Women's Bureau and union women emphasized lobbying for equal pay and minimum wage and maximum hour legislation. By the late 1960s, they would drop their opposition to the ERA as the feminist movement began to rise.

The Women's Bureau laid some of the groundwork for working women's feminism of the 1960s. The Bureau established a Labor

Advisory Committee (1945), which offered union women networking possibilities for shared concerns and tactical advice. It was most active between 1945 and 1953, and then revived in 1961, when Esther Peterson took over. Peterson was instrumental in convincing President John F. Kennedy to create a Commission for the Status of Women, something the Women's Bureau first called for in 1945 in its proposed Women's Status Act. Historians credit the Commission as a key foundation for the emergence of the feminist movement in the 1960s. Although relatively little came of the Women's Bureau or union women's call for better treatment for women workers during the war years, their efforts laid the groundwork for a more successful working women's feminism in the next decade and beyond (Documents 57 and 58).

CHALLENGES FOR WORKING WOMEN: FACTORY LIFE AND THE SECOND SHIFT

Most women in industry felt they earned their pay due to the hardships they endured. The hours were long and the work usually required physical stamina, if not always strength. Factories were loud and the work frequently dirty. Because plants operated without down time, women might find themselves on the swing shift (4 p.m. to midnight) or night duty (state laws against night work for women were often temporarily suspended). For women with children, night work could be desirable because they could split childcare duties with their husbands and be with their children during their waking hours, but it also led to disruptive sleep patterns and enhanced fatigue. Women, especially those who were among the first cohort to invade male work space, often faced hostility from resentful men.

Although it is difficult to document, as might be expected, women also experienced what we now call sexual harassment. Plants often staged formal beauty contests that sexualized women workers. Some women endured catcalls and whistles; others inappropriate touching and innuendos. There was little or no recourse for complaints about unwanted advances, and women usually had to solve the problem themselves. Although many may have just opted to ignore it, others, like shipyard worker Loena Ellis, fought back. When a man grabbed her by the ankle, she "just brought that hammer right down on his hard hat and knocked his glasses off and broke them. That's the only time anybody ever tried anything."[45]

Although working women were subject to unwanted sexual advances, many also found that wartime conditions offered them opportunities to expand their sexual horizons. With more money in their pockets, young people could enjoy more urban amusements, especially dancing at ballrooms and nightclubs where "jitterbugging" — a raucous dance — reflected the exuberant and sexy ambience of these clubs. Boomtowns, filled with young workers away from home, and cities with a large military presence created spaces for meeting sexual partners. One working woman explained that "Chicago was just humming, no matter where I went. The bars were jammed, and unless you were an absolute dog, you could pick up anyone you wanted to."[46] A small lesbian bar culture also emerged. Mona's in San Francisco catered to both civilians and women in the military. Pat Bond, a WAC (Women's Army Corps), described its appeal: "It was a sense of being somewhere finally where everybody was gay, not just you."[47] However, most lesbians apparently preferred to socialize in more private venues, in part to protect their reputations and, in the case of military women, to avoid detection.[48]

While many women could enjoy the fruits of wartime amusements, for most working women, the difficult conditions in the factories and shipyards were exacerbated by the complications of the second shift, the term scholars use to describe the work women do after they finish their paid employment for the day. Post-work hours could be hectic, especially for women with families. Although some women were able to participate in carpools to work, most had to rely upon overloaded public transportation systems that mean standing room only and delays. Housing was in short supply, making the lives of migrants to boomtowns and cities even more difficult. Many moved in with family members or roomed with coworkers (Documents 8, 9, and 31). African Americans' housing needs were even more difficult to meet as many landlords refused to rent to black workers, a situation that forced newcomers into already crowded housing in African American neighborhoods where buildings were often substandard and scarce. In some cities especially hard hit by the housing crisis, the federal government built housing projects, which were segregated. Housing designed for blacks lagged behind those intended for white workers.[49]

Coping with routine household chores in a limited amount of time was made all the more difficult by rationing of key food items (butter, sugar, coffee, and meat) and limited store hours (Document 29). In some communities, stores agreed to stay open late at least one night a week, but many women were frustrated in their efforts to feed and clothe themselves and their families. The War Manpower Commission urged magazines and newspapers to print articles offering advice to women on streamlined housekeeping and cooking, suggestions that rarely involved men sharing in household tasks. Certainly many men must have stepped up to assist, but few men or women seemed to have questioned a woman war worker's primary responsibility for the second shift. Working lives may have changed, but cultural assumptions remained largely unchanged.

Assumptions about the responsibility for childcare remained intact as well. During the war, working mothers were responsible for an estimated 1.5 million children under the age of six. Government agencies, including the WMC, the Women's Bureau, and the Children's Bureau, all expressed disapproval of mothers of young children in the workforce. In August 1942, the WMC issued a statement that "the first responsibility of women with young children in war as in peace is to give suitable care to their children."[50] But this sentiment deterred neither labor-hungry employers nor mothers eager for paid employment. Childcare, however, was a pressing concern.

Most families relied upon informal childcare. While some mothers might pay a neighbor to tend to their children, others drew upon family members (Documents 9, 13, and 31). Sisters, mothers, and grandmothers were pressed into service. Some oral history accounts reveal other strategies for migrant women who might leave their children behind with family members as they relocated in search of employment (Document 12). Less frequent, but still common, was the solution of shipyard worker Edna Hopkins, whose older schoolchildren shared some of the responsibility while she and her husband took different work shifts "so that one of us would be available."[51] And, according to a Women's Bureau survey conducted late in the war, many women "made no real provision" for childcare. In Seattle, for example, 25 percent of women questioned reported the absence of childcare plans.[52]

Faced with concern about absenteeism and unattended children, the federal government ultimately funded some childcare facilities. During the Depression, the Works Project Administration (WPA), a New Deal agency, had established centers to assist poor families. When wartime pressures created new demands, WPA nurseries shifted to care for "defense" children, and then in 1943, the Federal Works Agency (FWA) took over federal childcare services (Document 32). The FWA had been authorized by the Lanham Act of 1941 to assist defense communities in construction projects. Although it made no mention of childcare, a reference to "public services" became the justification to use federal resources for defense workers' families. The FWA required communities to apply for funds and to pay half of the costs.

Significantly, other federal government efforts at providing childcare did not succeed. Congress failed to pass a law known as the Thomas Bill, which would provide childcare for defense workers under the supervision primarily of the Children's Bureau (Document 33). The Thomas Bill authorized federal funding, but left the direction of the program to the individual states' education and children's committees. Commentary over the proposed law revealed hostility to the intrusion of government into family life and unwillingness to commit federal funds for such assistance. Women in the African American sorority Alpha Kappa Alpha opposed the bill because the sorority feared that Southern states would exclude black children. Under the FWA and the Lanham Act, about a tenth of childcare centers served African Americans and the sorority women feared these opportunities would be jeopardized under the Thomas Bill.[53] A key assumption of other critics was that children were a private matter, not one for public policy. And, repeatedly, the fear that working mothers endangered their children stymied efforts at a federal childcare law.

As the FWA created childcare facilities through the interpretation of existing legislation, it did so in an inhospitable climate. Although there were exceptions to this resistance, especially among women labor union leaders (see below and Document 25), government childcare centers from the beginning were viewed by some as necessary—and temporary—evils. Many cities were slow to request funding, although those like Portland, Oregon, with large migrant communities, were quicker off the mark. All told, 3,100 centers were created and served an estimated 150,000 children yearly. These centers charged 50 cents per child per day, a sum that could be prohibitive for large families.

Despite the significant need for childcare, many of these facilities were underutilized for a variety of reasons. They did not take children under two, and many offered no provision for after-school care. They were rarely located in buildings close to factories, thus requiring mothers to take crowded buses to drop children off before heading to work themselves, which added pressure to the second shift. Moreover, many centers did not open early enough for some schedules and were not useful for women on swing or night shifts. Finally, the underutilization may be chalked up to parents being unwilling to trust their children to strangers, especially those connected to a federal government so recently associated with helping the down-and-out in welfare programs. In the end, childcare under the Lanham Act was a short-lived experiment, as it was intended to be. Within days of the war ending, the FWA announced the end of funding, and by 1946 the centers were closed.[54]

There were other nondomestic options for childcare as well. Some commercial nurseries began operation, many of them poorly regulated and of dubious quality. Church groups and women's clubs sponsored some facilities for war workers' children. But the most interesting institutional alternative was the program developed in the Kaiser shipyards in Portland, Oregon, and Richmond, California (Document 34). Henry J. Kaiser was innovative in production methods, but also in programs to minimize absenteeism and labor turnover, a serious problem, especially among women and especially among mothers. Kaiser childcare centers received subsidies from the federal Maritime Bureau.

The centers, located adjacent to the yards, were well designed with children's needs in mind. Kaiser hired professional and progressive educators to run them and paid well over the scale to maximize quality and minimize turnover. The centers operated twenty-four hours a day and provided meals and recreation. They even offered a hot meal program for mothers to take home food for the family meal. Estimates are that the centers served about 1,000 children over the course of the war. Although highly successful, with war's end and the end of federal subsidies, Kaiser closed the centers.

The problems of working families have yet to be addressed by public policy. The war years were a time of missed opportunity. The ambivalent response to the need for childcare, rooted in part to resistance to mothers in the workforce, reveals the limits of World War II to transforming women's employment opportunities.

WOMEN IN THE ARMED SERVICES

One group of war workers did not have to worry about the second shift. Perhaps the most dramatic and controversial form of defense work for women was in the armed services. Certainly, military service is a unique type of employment that is often shaped by patriotic sentiments, but nonetheless it is wage labor and during World War II, it offered a key example of the ways in which working women seemed to be crossing the boundaries that had limited their opportunities. Given the association of the military with masculinity, it is not surpassing that there was resistance to enlisting women. Although Congresswoman Edith Nourse Rogers (Republican from Massachusetts) insisted on giving women equal opportunities to serve the country, conservative congressmen resisted, sure that women in the military would be a threat to the family and masculine identity. As one member of Congress asked,

"What has become of the manhood in America that we have to call on our women to do what has ever been the duty of men?"[55]

But military leaders quickly recognized that women could perform a variety of functions that would permit more men to take up combat roles and serve overseas. This realization reflected, too, a major change in the nature of warfare, where technological and administrative support became essential elements. During World War II, 38.8 percent of male soldiers served in noncombat roles.[56] Thus despite opposition by conservatives who feared that military women would become "ersatz" (or fake) men, in May 1942 Congress created the Women's Army Auxiliary Corps (WAAC), with the "auxiliary" terminology a clear indication that women's military work was assumed to be secondary. The group became the Women's Army Corps (WAC) and officially part of the army sixteen months later. The WAC was the largest group of enlisted women (140,000); followed by the naval Women Accepted for Volunteer Emergency Service (WAVES; 100,000), Marine Corps Reserves (23,000), and the Coast Guard Women's Reserve (13,000). In addition, 60,000 women served in the Army Nurse Corps and another 14,000 in the Navy Nurse Corps. Finally, 1,000 women were members of the Women's Airforce Service Pilots (WASP), who were civilian employees, but worked closely with the military. [57]

Each service had slightly different requirements, but in general women needed to have high school degrees, and officers needed college degrees or a combination of college and work experience. Nurses generally had a few years of experience, and 40 percent had college educations. Married women could enlist, but usually not those with minor children. Women of color formed a small component of women in the military, and for many ethnic minorities — Filipinas, Mexican American, and Chinese and Japanese Americans (although not until they had submitted to loyalty tests) — military service was a means of demonstrating one's "Americanness" (Documents 39–41).

As was the case for civilian workers, African American women faced discrimination in the military. Mostly serving in the WAC, where they never constituted more than 10 percent of the force (Documents 37, 38, and 49), they were totally excluded from the U.S. Navy until late in the war, when four black women became members of the WAVES. With the exception of the WAVES, black women, like black men, served in segregated units and were usually assigned to duties below their skills and educational levels and rarely offered any opportunities for specialized or technical training. As nurses, they were permitted to treat only black soldiers and prisoners of war.

Organizations like the National Association for the Advancement of Colored People (NAACP) and the National Council of Negro Women—the latter headed by Mary McLeod Bethune, who took special interest in black WACs—repeatedly drew attention to the racial discrimination black women faced in the military, but they made little progress. Oveta Culp Hobby, the Texas newspaperwoman who headed up the WAC, initially refused to send black women abroad. Pressure from civil rights groups, however, did lead to one unit of black WACs serving in Europe (the 6888th, led by Charity Adams) in 1944 (Document 37). And, in a highly publicized court-martial case of four African American WACs who staged a strike to protest the way in which they were limited to menial labor at Fort Devens in Massachusetts, pressure from the black press and civil rights activists induced the army to rescind the women's convictions (Document 38). The reversal, however, did not lead to correcting the discrimination black women faced at Fort Devens or elsewhere.[58]

Whatever their ethnicity or race, women enlisted for a variety of reasons. Patriotism was important, but so too was the opportunity for adventure and independence. Some hoped for training that would aid them after the war. And since many enlistees came from rural areas or small towns where there were no defense industry jobs, military service offered steady work that was otherwise unavailable (Document 39).[59]

Much of the media tended to present military women in stereotypical and flippant fashion. They were either too featherbrained to be efficient or too masculine to be women. Cartoons featuring one or the other multiplied, and the message was often that "femininity and soldiering were incompatible."[60] And magazine articles often spent more time describing the women's uniforms than reporting on their work and experience (Documents 35 and 36). This sort of representation was particularly annoying to Oveta Hobby of the WAC, who strove for respectful and fair treatment of her troops. Nonetheless, her vision of the WAC was in many ways conventional. As one historian explained, "[S]he viewed the women's corps as a temporary entity which should be disbanded when the war was over and whose members should be returned to their families and their primary duties as wives and mothers."[61] Hobby, in keeping with male military leaders' expectations, assumed that WACs would serve primarily in clerical jobs to release men for combat.

And indeed, despite anxieties about women in uniform undermining the gender order, most military women served in jobs that were conventionally "women's work" (Documents 39, 44, and 45). One general's comment that "we have found difficulty in getting enlisted men to perform tedious duties anywhere near as well as women would do it"[62] was a telling statement about the views of women's abilities for certain types of work. Significantly, even when WASPs took on "men's" work, piloting in noncombat roles, they were refused military status (Document 47). Their contributions were needed, but male pilots resisted the notion of women's equality that military rank would imply.

Despite the tendency to steer women toward the realms of "women's work," among the WAC and other organizations, some women did perform work nonconventional for their gender. Many military women were truck drivers, mechanics, and parachute riggers. Aptitude testing placed an elite group of women in code-breaking units whose work complemented that of civilian code breakers. Women were also likely to receive training in communication technology, a decision that was related to women's long-standing dominance among telephone operators. For the most part, however, outside the nursing corps, women performed the clerical work that a large bureaucratic military desperately needed. As one historian summed up the nature of military women's work, "the great majority of service women were engaged in the traditional female areas of office work, communications, and health care."[63]

Military service took some adjustment because of the regimentation and the problem of adjusting to a new environment and barracks life, especially for those women who went abroad (Documents 45 and 46). Nurses in particular were exposed to the trauma of war medicine and often were stationed close to the front and near danger. Another hardship military women faced was the widespread rumors that they were sexually immoral (Documents 39, 42, and 43). In 1943 especially, stories multiplied that WACs in particular were virtually prostitutes for military men or that they were lesbians. Nurses were less likely subjects of such rumors, but they were not immune either. Investigating the origins of these stories, the Federal Bureau of Investigation decided that the rumors were spread by servicemen hostile to women because their role in the military was to take the place of men so that they might be freed for combat. Believing that the stories were hurting recruitment of women, military leaders downplayed the argument that women were replacements for men. At the same time, they were careful to emphasize military women's femininity and sexual morality.

The rumors exacerbated preexisting anxieties about sexual misconduct among women in the armed services. Certainly military life offered both heterosexual and homosexual women a degree of freedom to explore their sexuality away from the restraints of family and community. Concern about the services' reputation led military leaders, especially in the WAC, to establish policies designed to limit women's sexual opportunities. While WAC leadership worried about promiscuity in general, the greatest anxiety focused on lesbians. Some women were able to conduct affairs with other women discreetly, without much harassment, but women who appeared "mannish" — a euphemism for lesbian — through haircut, mannerisms, or language, were routinely subject to investigation. WAC officials urged recruiters to be alert to women with mannish tendencies or to those who indicated that they wanted to enlist to "be with other girls."[64]

Although officers might investigate individual women who were rumored to be lesbian, the WAC also conducted a few confidential investigations at military locales where lesbians were thought to be numerous. At the WAC training center at Fort Oglethorpe, Georgia, for example, a 1944 hearing resulted in a number of forced resignations and the hospitalization of five women to undergo psychiatric evaluation and treatment. At the hearing, the women were subjected to humiliating questions about romantic desire and sexual practices. Other witnesses were asked to provide evidence about the accused women's behavior. Although the report was perhaps more revealing about the anxiety surrounding lesbians in the military than it was about lesbian experience, nonetheless the women's voices do emerge in the hundreds of pages of documents created by the hearing board and suggest that many women could and did find opportunities to love other WACs (Document 43).[65]

The report also made it clear that appearance and sexuality outside the conventions of "femininity" was risky business. Both lesbians and straight women were discharged based on often flimsy evidence of sexual misconduct. Anything other than an honorable discharge would hurt women's future employment prospects and disqualified them for GI benefits. Beyond the damage done to individuals, these policies reveal pervasive fears about women's sexual agency in the context of the disruption of wartime. Military women became a lightning rod for concerns that women crossing boundaries in the army and in the workplace were challenging the gender, and specifically, the sexual order.[66]

THE END OF THE WAR AND BEYOND

The anxieties about women challenging the gender order in their war work would become strikingly clear as the war came to an end in August 1945. Many working women suddenly experienced a dramatic shrinking of their opportunities. In just a few months, between June and September 1945, 25 percent of women in factories lost their jobs. Between 1945 and 1946, the number of women in the workforce decreased dramatically, from 19,170,000 to 16,896,000.[67] Gladys Belcher, a welder in California, for example, had looked ahead to her postwar employment opportunities by taking night classes to be certified in a variety of welding techniques. Laid off at the end of the war, she took her qualifications to a job interview, only to be told, "You're a woman." Despite her impressive skills, the company would not hire her. Belcher, a widow, spent the rest of her working life as a school cook. Her story exemplifies what happened to most women who had briefly breached the barrier of the sex-segregated labor market.[68]

At the end of the war, most male union leaders and employers showed little interest in protecting women's stake in their new jobs. Ida DuMars, the general supervisor of women workers at a Boeing plant in Washington, and presumably speaking for the company, declared that women "will go back to their homes, and to their beauty parlors and banks and they love the idea." Tellingly, she added, "Those who intend to keep on working, know their wages will be smaller, but they expect it and don't mind."[69] As DuMars implied, those who continued to work did so for the most part in jobs traditionally held by women. This return to sex-segregated patterns was reinforced by the policies of the United States Employment Service, which during the high unemployment of the immediate postwar years, usually required women, but not men, to accept lower-status jobs rather than persist in looking for jobs commensurate with their new skills while receiving unemployment benefits.

Military women's postwar expectations were different from those of their industrial counterparts (Document 54). Women had signed up for the duration of the war, and relatively few expected to make the armed forces a career. Those who served abroad, especially in stressful environments, were eager to return home and to civilian life. For some women, particularly officers, the training and experience they received proved useful in postwar work. Nurses, however, were often disappointed. Civilian work paid poorly, and they had few opportunities for promotion. Within two years of war's end, 38 percent of nurses had left the profession. Military women did enjoy one benefit, however.

Those who had served in a branch of the armed forces were eligible for GI benefits (including education, housing and small business loans, and unemployment compensation) established by the Servicemen's Readjustment Act of 1944. Of the 350,000 women who served, 65,000 attained further education through these benefits. Women pilots in the WASP were not so fortunate. Because they were not considered members of the military, not only were they unable to find civilian jobs as pilots, they were also denied benefits. It was not until after vigorous lobbying of Congress that they received veteran status in 1977.

These discouraging stories are not to say that the war had no impact on employment patterns. After World War II, more women worked than ever before. By 1950, 29 percent of women worked in contrast to 25.4 percent in 1940. And more married women found employment in the workforce than ever before (31 percent of the female workforce in 1940, in contrast to 47 percent in 1950).[70] But for the most part, the broad occupational distribution of women's work was much the same as it had been in 1940. In 1940 about half of all women workers had been in low-waged service, sales, or clerical jobs. Another 20 percent were in low-paid manufacturing jobs, mostly in textiles and clothing industries. In 1950, those numbers were 58 percent and 19 percent, respectively.

As women's employment went up in service, sales, and clerical jobs, their numbers dropped in agricultural and domestic work, which benefited African Americans and other women of color in particular. For example, almost 60 percent of black women workers in 1940 had been in domestic service, while in 1950 that percentage dropped to 41 percent. In agriculture, the percentages shifted from 12 to 7.5 percent.[71] Women of color still faced a racially segmented labor market, but the war opened up more desirable jobs (as clerks, factory operatives, and sales personnel) than had been available in the past (Document 49) and, moreover, undoubtedly raised expectations about future opportunities in the workforce.

The cultural context for the limitations placed on women's opportunities emerged very clearly in the months surrounding the war's end. The media extensively covered the Women's Bureau's commentary on the war's impact on American women's employment and its call for more equity for women workers. The Bureau's survey of ten defense industry centers revealed that 75 percent of those working in 1944–1945 wanted to keep their job at war's end (Document 48). Newspapers and magazines also printed stories by and about women who were determined to stay in the workforce and who complained about the discrimination their sex experienced (Documents 49–51, and 54).

And, as we have seen, women union activists were also outspoken in their struggle for more fair treatment. But more pervasive in the media coverage was the flip side — accounts that insisted both that women wanted to return to the home and that social order and prosperity required their commitment to domesticity (Documents 52, 53, and 55). It was these ideas about women's proper place in the home and the importance of clear-cut gender roles for both men and women that would dominate mainstream culture in the postwar era. If not all women lived their lives according to the "feminine mystique," as feminist Betty Friedan later termed it, this ideology helped to maintain a labor environment for women that devalued their work and limited their opportunities.

World War II encouraged more women to work — during and after the war. It helped, too, to encourage more wives and mothers to seek paid employment. And, it opened up more opportunity for women of color, whose options had been largely agricultural and domestic work. It also sparked civil rights activism among African American women that would continue into the postwar era. But cultural notions of women's place in the home — a view so clearly emphasized when the WMC stressed the temporary nature of women's war work — meant that women continued to work in devalued and low-paid "women's work." Women labor leaders would increasingly challenge discrimination in the labor market — a challenge certainly rooted in their wartime experiences. It would be more than a decade, however, before the feminist movement, which included many union women, mounted a more sustained — if imperfectly realized — challenge to women's inequality in the workforce.

NOTES

[1]James J. Kimble and Lester C. Olson, "Visual Rhetoric Representing Rosie the Riveter: Myth and Misconception in J. Howard Miller's 'We Can Do It!' Poster," *Rhetoric and Public Affairs* 9 (Winter 2006): 551. For Miller's poster, see http://americanhistory .si.edu/collections/search/object/nmah_538122; for Rockwell's, see http://www .curtispublishing.com. For the *New Yorker Cover* by Abigail Gray Swartz, see the February 6, 2017, issue.

[2]Lynn Y. Weiner, *From Working Girl to Working Mother: The Female Labor Force in the United States, 1820–1980* (Chapel Hill: University of North Carolina Press, 1985), 27.

[3]Julia Kirk Blackwelder, *Now Hiring: The Feminization of Work in the United States, 1900–1995* (College Station: Texas A&M University Press, 1997), chapter 1; Ruth Milkman, "Organizing the Sexual Division of Labor: Historical Perspectives on 'Women's Work' and the American Labor Movement," in Ruth Milkman, *On Gender, Labor, and Inequality* (Urbana: University of Illinois Press, 2016), 79–118.

[4]Nancy Woloch, *A Class by Herself: Protective Laws for Women Workers, 1890s–1990s* (Princeton, N.J.: Princeton University Press, 2015), chapters 1–4; Alice Kessler-Harris,

Out to Work: A History of Wage-Earning Women in the United States (New York: Oxford University Press, 2003), 184–86.

[5]Lynn Dumenil, *The Second Line of Defense: American Women and World War I* (Chapel Hill: University of North Carolina Press, 2017), chapter 4.

[6]Lynn Dumenil, *The Modern Temper: American Culture and Society in the 1920s* (New York: Hill and Wang, 1995), 122.

[7]Susan Ware, *Holding Their Own: American Women in the 1930s* (Boston: G. K. Hall, 1982), chapter 2.

[8]Maureen Honey, *Creating Rosie the Riveter: Class, Gender, and Propaganda during World War II* (Amherst: University of Massachusetts Press, 1984); Leila J. Rupp, *Mobilizing Women for War: German and American Propaganda, 1939–1945* (Princeton, N.J.: Princeton University Press, 1978), 137–66.

[9]Melissa A. McEuen, *Making War, Making Women: Femininity and Duty on the American Home Front, 1941–1945* (Athens: University of Georgia Press, 2011); Dona B. Knaff, *Beyond Rosie the Riveter: Women of World War II in American Popular Graphic Art* (Lawrence: University Press of Kansas, 2012); Robert B. Westbrook, "'I Want a Girl, Just Like the Girl That Married Harry James': American Women and the Problem of Political Obligation," in Westbrook, *Why We Fought: Forging American Obligations in World War II* (Washington, D.C.: Smithsonian Books, 2010), 67–92.

[10]Kathleen A. Laughlin, *Women's Work and Public Policy: A History of the Women's Bureau, U.S. Department of Labor* (Boston: Northeastern University Press, 2000), 3–40.

[11]Blackwelder, *Now Hiring*, 124.

[12]Kessler-Harris, *Out to Work*, 276.

[13]United States Department of Labor Women's Bureau and Mary Elizabeth Pidgeon, *Changes in Women's Employment during the War: Special Bulletin No. 20 of the Women's Bureau* (Washington, D.C.: U.S. Government Printing Office, 1944), 17.

[14]Maureen Honey, ed., *Bitter Fruit: African American Women in World War II* (Columbia: University of Missouri Press, 1999), 1–34.

[15]Richard Santillán, "Rosita the Riveter: Midwest Mexican American Women during World War II, 1941–1945," *Perspectives in Mexican American Studies* 2 (1989): 132.

[16]Vicki L. Ruiz, *Cannery Women, Cannery Lives: Mexican Women, Unionization, and the California Food Processing Industry* (Albuquerque: University of New Mexico Press, 1978), 69–86.

[17]Elizabeth R. Escobedo, *From Coveralls to Zoot Suits: The Lives of Mexican American Women on the World War II Homefront* (Chapel Hill: University of North Carolina Press, 2013), 101.

[18]Grace Mary Gouveia, "'We Also Serve': American Indian Women's Role in World War II," *Michigan Historical Review* 20 (Fall 1994): 153–82; "Chilocco's Defense Class," *The Indian School Journal* 42 (November 13, 1942): 1.

[19]Valerie Matsumoto, "Japanese American Women during World War II," in *Unequal Sisters: A Multi-Cultural Reader in U.S. Women's History*, ed. Ellen Carol DuBois and Vicki L. Ruiz (New York: Routledge, 1990), 378.

[20]Magazine Division, Office of War Information, "Magazine War Guide for June–July 1943," March 17, 1943, Records of the Office of War Information (RG 208), National Archives Box, 1700.

[21]Magazine Division, Office of War Information, "Reports on Women at Work," June 1943, Records of the Office of War Information (RG 208), National Archives Box, 1700.

[22]United States Department of Labor Women's Bureau and Mary Elizabeth Pidgeon, *Changes in Women's Occupations during the War: Special Bulletin No. 20 of the Women's Bureau* (Washington, D.C.: U.S. Government Printing Office, 1944), 9.

[23]Laura Micheletti Puaca, *Searching for Scientific Womanpower: Technocratic Feminism and the Politics of National Security, 1940–1980* (Chapel Hill: University of North Carolina Press, 2014), 29–30.

[24]Ibid., 32.

[25]Ibid.

[26]Ibid., 9–41.

[27]Weiner, *From Working Girl to Working Mother*, 95.

[28]Ruth Milkman, *Gender at Work: The Dynamics of Segregation by Sex during World War II* (Urbana: University of Illinois Press, 1987), 9.

[29]Ibid., 74–77.

[30]Kessler-Harris, *Out to Work*, 290. Hard figures are difficult to come by, and historians offer competing estimates. See also Mark Aldrich, "The Gender Gap in Earnings during World War II: New Evidence," *Industrial and Labor Relations Review* 42 (April 1989): 415–29.

[31]Amy Kesselman, *Fleeting Opportunities: Women Shipyard Workers in Portland and Vancouver during World War II and Reconversion* (Albany: State University of New York Press, 1987), 29.

[32]Aldrich, "The Gender Gap in Earnings during World War II," 424.

[33]Kimberle Crenshaw, "Mapping the Margins: Intersectionality, Identity Politics, and Violence against Women of Color," *Stanford Law Review* 43 (July 1991): 1241–99.

[34]Andrew E. Kersten, *Race, Jobs, and the War: The FEPC in the Midwest, 1941–46* (Urbana: University of Illinois Press, 2007).

[35]Karen Tucker Anderson, "Last Hired, First Fired: Black Women Workers during World War II," *Journal of American History* 69 (June 1982): 84.

[36]Eileen Boris, "'You Wouldn't Want One of 'Em Dancing with Your Wife': Racialized Bodies on the Job in World War II," *American Quarterly* 50 (1998): 77–108.

[37]Katherine Turk, "'A Fair Chance to Do My Part of Work': Black Women, War Work, and Rights Claims at the Kingsbury Ordnance Plant," *Indiana Magazine of History* 108 (2012): 236–37.

[38]Megan Taylor Schockley, *"We, Too, Are Americans": African American Women in Detroit and Richmond, 1940–1954* (Urbana: University of Illinois Press, 2004), 92.

[39]Milkman, *Gender at Work*, 2 and 85.

[40]Nancy F. Gabin, *Feminism in the Labor Movement: Women and the United Auto Workers, 1935–1975* (Ithaca, N.Y.: Cornell University Press, 1990), 63.

[41]Ibid., 101.

[42]Dorothy Sue Cobble, *The Other Women's Movement: Workplace Justice and Social Rights in Modern America* (Princeton, N.J.: Princeton University Press, 2004), 17.

[43]Ibid., 57.

[44]Ibid., 7.

[45]Kesselman, *Fleeting Opportunities*, 63.

[46]Elaine Tyler May, "Rosie the Riveter Gets Married," in *The War in American Culture: Society and Consciousness during World War II*, ed. Lewis A. Erenberg and Susan E. Hirsch (Chicago: University of Chicago Press, 1996), 128.

[47]Leisa D. Meyer, *Creating G.I. Jane: Sexuality and Power in the Women's Army Corps during World War II* (New York: Columbia University Press, 1996), 167.

[48]Allan Berube, *Coming Out under Fire: The History of Gay Men and Women in World War II* (New York: Free Press, 1990), 113–16; Lillian Faderman, *Odd Girls and Twilight Lovers: A History of Lesbian Life in Twentieth-Century America* (New York: Penguin, 1991), 127.

[49]Rhonda Williams, *Politics of Public Housing: Black Women's Struggles against Urban Inequality* (New York: Oxford University Press, 2004), 51–56.

[50]Kesselman, *Fleeting Opportunities*, 68.

[51]Ibid., 71.

[52]Karen Anderson, *Wartime Women: Sex Roles, Family Relations, and the Status of Women during World War II* (Westport, Conn.: Greenwood Press, 1981), 144.

[53]"Wartime Care and Protection of Children of Employed Mothers," Hearing before the Committee on Education and Labor, United States Congress, 78th Cong., 1st Sess. on S.876. GP, 1943, 76.

[54]Susan E. Riley, "Caring for Rosie's Children: Federal Child Care Policies in the World War II Era," *Polity* 26 (Summer 1994): 655–75; Kesselman, *Fleeting Opportunities*, 65–89.

[55]M. Michaela Hampf, "'Dykes' or 'Whores': Sexuality and the Women's Army Corps in the United States during World War II," *Women's Studies International Forum* 27 (2004): 13.

[56]"Research Starters: US Military by the Numbers," The National WWII Museum, accessed January 7, 2019, https://www.nationalww2museum.org/students-teachers/student-resources/research-starters/research-starters-us-military-numbers.

[57]Susan M. Hartmann, *The Home Front and Beyond: American Women in the 1940s* (Boston: Twayne, 1982), 31–32.

[58]Sandra M. Bolzenius, *Glory in Their Spirit: How Four Black Women Took on the Army during World War II* (Urbana: University of Illinois Press, 2018).

[59]D'Ann Campbell, *Women at War with America: Private Lives in a Patriotic Era* (Cambridge, Mass.: Harvard University Press, 1984), 17–62; Hartmann, *The Home Front and Beyond*, 31–52.

[60]Christina M. Knopf, "'Hey Soldier!—Your Slip is Showing!' Militarism vs. Femininity in World War II Comic Pages and Books," in *The 10 Cent War: Comic Books, Propaganda, and World War II* (Jackson: University Press of Mississippi, 2016), 30.

[61]Meyer, *Creating G.I. Jane*, 17.

[62]Hartmann, *American Women in the 1940s*, 34.

[63]Ibid., 37.

[64]Meyer, *Creating G.I. Jane*, 157.

[65]Ibid., 173–77.

[66]Ibid., 33–70.

[67]Department of Labor Women's Bureau and Pidgeon, *Employment of Women in the Early Postwar Period*, 2, 5.

[68]*Life and Times of Rosie the Riveter* (1980), documentary by Connie Field.

[69]Anderson, *Wartime Women*, 162.

[70]United States Department of Labor Women's Bureau and Mary Elizabeth Pidgeon, *Changes in Women's Occupations, 1940–1950: Women's Bureau Bulletin No. 253* (Washington, D.C.: U.S. Government Printing Office, 1954), 7.

[71]Blackwelder, *Now Hiring*, 154.

PART TWO

The Documents

1

Propaganda: The Campaign to Recruit Womanpower

Although a number of agencies participated in the "womanpower" campaign to recruit women to the workforce, the most important was the Office of War Information's Bureau of Campaigns, which cooperated closely with the War Advertising Council, established by the advertising industry in November 1941. The bureau distributed a monthly "War Guide for Advertisers" conveying information and ideas about war needs to be incorporated in commercial advertising. Another vital agency was the OWI's Magazine Bureau, established in June 1942. The Magazine Bureau disseminated a bimonthly "Magazine War Guide," which provided detailed information, images, and story and article suggestions about the war to the nation's magazines.

Compliance with government recommendations about publicity was voluntary, but advertisers and magazine editors were quick to incorporate the information and ideas they received from government agencies as a means of informing the public and conveying their own patriotic commitment to the war effort. In considering the documents that follow, what rationales did the womanpower campaign offer to encourage women to take on war jobs? What were its assumptions about women's aspirations in these jobs? Why do you suppose the material designed for African American women (Document 7) was so different from that directed to white women?

OFFICE OF WAR INFORMATION

Women in the War . . . for the Final Push to Victory
1943

*This document prepared by the Magazine Bureau was typical of the
material distributed to encourage magazines to promote women's war
work. In this extract, the Bureau addresses potential resistance of
women to civilian work as well as to military service.*

Women in Production and in Essential Civilian Work

The War Manpower Commission estimates that there will need to be
hundreds of thousands of additional women workers in 1944 to meet
the requirements for war production and essential civilian jobs. Due to
the present rate of turnover and the large number of part-time workers
among applicants, hundreds of thousands of women must be recruited
to maintain and increase the necessary net supply. . . .

Appeals should therefore:

(1) Dramatize the vital role of the 17,000,000 women now helping to
speed victory in war plants, in essential civilian jobs, and in the armed
services.

(2) Advise women that when the Nation is at war, women must work
as men must fight.

(3) Stress the fact that women are urgently needed in some areas
and in some plants—and not in others. Women must be directed to
their local USES[1] office to find out local needs.

(4) Create a sense of urgency in the appeal by relating it to the final
push to victory.

(5) Tell women that war jobs are not always immediately available
in every community—but that it is up to them to find their war jobs
through their local USES [office] instead of waiting for a war job to find
them.

---

[1]United States Employment Service.

Office of War Information, "Women in the War . . . for the final push to victory," 1943,
Records of the Office of War Information (RG 208), National Archives, Box 587, 2–4.

The resistance of women to war jobs should be met as directly as possible

SOME OF THE RESISTANCE TO WAR JOBS	SOME OF THE ANSWERS
1. "I read in the paper that they are letting women go in some factories. Does that mean that the war is nearly over and that it is no longer urgent for women to leave their homes and go to work?"	Frequent adjustments in production schedules result from changing battle front conditions. These cause sharp rises in production in some localities and reductions in others. The local USES can advise best on the local situation.
2. The work is too tiring.	For a few weeks, yes. But war jobs are matched to physical capacities wherever possible. War work is not easy, but necessary and satisfying.
3. The jobs are monotonous, boring.	So are many household jobs. In most plants, talking on the job is not prohibited. In many plants, music entertains workers at their machines. Rest periods, lunch hours, cafeterias and rest room facilities have been planned on a scientific basis.
4. I have never worked in a factory. I know nothing about machines.	Many war factory jobs are very similar to running a sewing machine or vacuum cleaner, assembling a meat grinder, sewing by hand, and other familiar household tasks. War jobs for women are easy to pick up. Most use skills already acquired. Besides, war plants and government-sponsored vocational schools give free training. In some cases women are paid while learning.

* * * * *

Some of the resistance to essential civilian jobs

1. How do I know it's a job that will help the war effort?	Any job that helps maintain essential civilian production or services—or any jobs that releases a man or another woman for military service or war plant work, is a war job.

2. I am doing volunteer work. Isn't that enough?	Volunteer work is fine—but it's not enough if a woman can take a full-time war job. The final push to victory calls for an 8-hour day for every woman who can manage it. Volunteer work should be supplementary to, not instead of, a job.
3. I don't need the money. What will my friends think?	A pay check for the woman who doesn't need it is honorable recognition for her help in the final push to victory—in a job that may not be pleasant or easy but which someone must do. The pay check can be turned into war bonds and so help the country both with work and money.
4. How can I handle the responsibilities of a job and my home and family, too?	The Nation owes a special debt of gratitude to the thousands of women who have rearranged their household duties to spend eight hours a day on the war production line or in essential civilian work. Many communities have also made adjustments—to meet the needs of workers and help to keep them on their jobs, shopping hours have been rearranged, transportation, banking hours, etc.

Women in Uniform

The over-all strength of the Women's Reserves of the Armed Service is approximately 130,000. Although their quotas for 1944 are much less than the need for women in the civilian war effort, it is a much more difficult requirement to meet because women of America have not responded in sufficient numbers to the many appeals for Women in Uniform.

This division of the program must therefore not only be equal in scope and weight to that of the civilian division but in many instances it must have special emphasis. . . .

Surveys made by the Services show that the resistances toward interest in the Women's Reserves are basic and common to all branches of the service. For this reason, all appeals should attempt to overcome one or all of the common reasons why women do not "join up" regardless of the particular service mentioned in any one program.

The appeals *heretofore* have tended to stress *only* such points as: the jobs done by women in uniform are vital to the war effort; that skills learned in the Service will have post-war advantage; that women will work side by side with men; that they will release a man to fight; that they will learn to drill and live in barracks and accustom themselves to Spartan comforts as men do.

While any and all of these appeals have their place and are useful in a recruitment program, they should first be supported by information that will overcome the resistance towards "joining up."

The basic reasons why women do not enter the Armed Forces indicate that they believe that such a life will change their fundamental ways of living as women. The essential error, however, has *not* been one of commission, but of omission.

Women have *not* been told in national publicity that military service does not destroy their femininity nor detract from it. There has *not* been sufficient emphasis on the fact that women in the Armed Forces are respected as women, and that they are not remolded into some other kind of half-male, half-female hybrid.

Women have been educated and continually encouraged not only to remain feminine, but to try and become "more so." They accordingly cannot be expected to respond to appeals which, through misplaced emphasis on uniforms and on comparisons with soldiers and sailors, suggest that they are regarded and treated as other than feminine. It is impossible to try to persuade them to adopt a life in which they believe that masculine instead of feminine customs will control their temperament and actions. While the primary motive for enlistment should be the patriotic one — to help in the war effort . . . the Reserves not only encourage but provide feminine interest and comforts to be enjoyed in leisure hours.

* * * * *

Here are the five basic resistances with some of the answers which this program should try to overcome:

1. RESISTANCES	SOME OF THE ANSWERS
1. Men disapprove of women in uniform.	Women in uniform are no less feminine than before they enlisted. Feminine interests are encouraged among women in the services. Their work is of the kind that women do in civilian life. They "date," dance, and go to parties, and have opportunities for feminine comforts and diversion in leisure hours.

Women in uniform have won the approval of their communities, the respect of their commanding officers, the friendship of the men they work with, and the admiration of men who knew them in civilian life.

In the service they gain a sympathetic understanding of the attitudes of the men who are fighting this war today and will build the homes of tomorrow. This understanding goes hand in hand with a femininity that remains unchanged. Actually they develop new poise and charm.

2. I don't want to be regimented.

The women's military services are vastly different from military service for men. Training periods are really indoctrination periods in which women learned the policies of the service branch, and are much like getting acquainted with any new job. Military drills provide the women with poise and a feeling of "belonging."

3. My parents won't let me join.

Parents of girls in uniform have learned that the services give invaluable training in skills useful in peacetime occupations, that special provisions have been made for the women's well-being and comfort, that organized recreation is provided. Most parents are proud of their daughters in uniform.

4. Adjustments would be too difficult.

Like a group of girls entering school or college, women in the armed services almost invariably find their new life interesting and stimulating. They see "new faces and new places" and associate with other women. They make friends quickly. And those who have been lonely in their home towns, with so many friends away, gain new companionships and absorbing interests that make life more worth living than ever before.

| 5. The pay is low compared with civilian jobs. | This is not true when food and quarters are taking into account in addition to base pay. When a girl is enlisted into the armed services, she gets approximately $50 a month base pay plus a food and quarters allowance if she provides her own room and board. This totals about $142.00 per month or a total "salary" of $32 per week in the lowest rank. Promotions can increase this to above $200 per month in enlisted status. |
| | In addition, clothing, medical and dental care, and special training are free. |

2

LIFE MAGAZINE

Cover Featuring a Woman Steel Worker

August 9, 1943

Magazines and newspapers responded to the requests for coverage of women working in defense. In August 1943, Life *magazine commissioned renowned photographer Margaret Bourke-White to document steel workers in Gary, Indiana. Bourke-White herself embodied the ways in which World War II allowed women to transgress work boundaries: She was the nation's first female war photojournalist. In keeping with suggestions from the Office of War Information, the photo essay included photographs of women engaged in various strenuous jobs and the accompanying text stressed the novelty of women's work, but also emphasized their ability. In addition to the images for the photo essay, Bourke-White's photo of steel worker Ann Zarik wearing goggles and hard at work at her job in the mill appeared on the magazine's cover.*

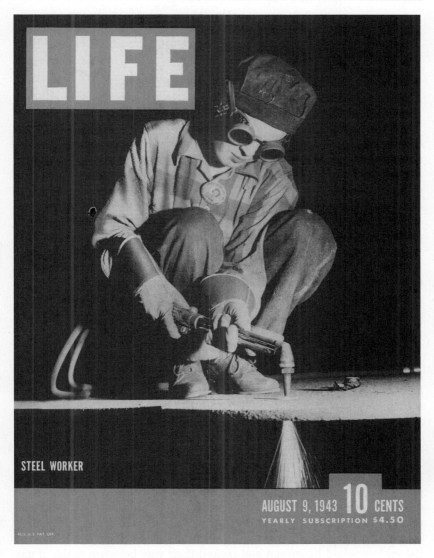

Photo by Margaret Bourke-White/The LIFE Premium Collection/Getty Images

3

PHYLLIS DUGANNE

When the Boys Come Home

July 17, 1943

---

*At the encouragement of the Magazine Bureau, the promotion of
womanpower for war also appeared in magazine fiction. The Saturday
Evening Post, for example, published numerous romantic short stories
about factory workers and military women. They invariably featured
illustrations of beautiful women, often dressed in work clothes or
military uniforms. For the following story, the accompanying picture
depicted the heroine in very feminine civilian clothes.*

---

*[At the beginning of the story, the soldier, Pete, depicts his fiancée, Marilyn,
as helpless.]*

"She was the ideal of what every man in the armed forces fought
for—to preserve her world and to return to her in it. . . . Win the War to
Keep Marilyn Spoiled—and Petted."

*[As the story continues, Pete is not happy to learn that Marilyn is training
to be a welder in a defense plant. And when he returns home on leave,
he is further disconcerted to see women doing men's work and unhappy
because Marilyn is too busy to spend much time with him. He then stops
by the training facility to pick up Marilyn and encounters her instructor,
Mr. Freeman.]*

Daniel Freeman talked smoothly and proudly as they went from room
to room. "Over eleven hundred trained workers graduated into defense
jobs." He picked up a metal object. "We made this here. Milling-machine
vise. This is a cutter." His capable hands held up another part. "Make all
our own tools. That girl over there is making a vise screw." They went
into the blueprint-reading room, the tracing class. They descended to
the whitewashed basement and picked their way between tanks of gas
and wooden crates. "Here's the welding."

Marilyn did not look up. Her blue eyes were hidden behind thick
dark glasses, and sparks flew upward from the acetylene torch in her

---

Phyllis Duganne, "When the Boys Come Home," *Saturday Evening Post,* July 17, 1943,
26, 27, 86, 88–90.

48

right hand. The steel rod in her left hand was steady; her tiny figure in blue overalls and a blue jacket was motionless and intent.

Daniel Freeman was holding out a pair of glasses. "Go over and watch her, if you like. She's getting quite expert."

Pete took off his hat and put on the glasses. Still Marilyn had not looked up. He stood beside her, watching the dribbling line of molten metal, like a decoration on a birthday cake squeezed from a cook's pastry tube. She completed the length of a square of practice steel and looked up. . . .

"Darling! I didn't hear you! I'm so glad you came. She shoved the glasses up to her forehead, just below the bright sheen of her hair. Have you met Mr. Freeman?"

He nodded, with a sudden lump crowding the walls of his throat. . . .

[They return to her house.]

They went together to the kitchen. She looked childlike, yet very feminine, in her overalls. She was tiny, but no one would mistake her for a boy. . . .

Win the War to Keep Marilyn Safe. She had been fortunate and happy but she had never been spoiled, and nothing was going to spoil her. Certainly not marriage.

"What about having a wedding tomorrow?" he asked.

She slipped from her perch on the kitchen table and went into his arms. "Oh, Pete, yes!" she agreed.

He stroked her hair back from her forehead and looked into her eager, happy eyes. She was only nineteen, but she was old enough. She was old enough for anything she had to face. She could work in a factory or do anything the country needed her to do, but when he returned and when the boys came home—she would be waiting in a pretty dress, with flowers in her hair.

4

Woodbury Facial Soap Advertisement Depicting Femininity and Romance for a Boeing Plant Worker

1943

Advertising executives, under the guidance of the War Advertising Council, wanted to demonstrate their and their clients' patriotism by promoting national war aims in advertising. Many of these manufacturers had converted their production from consumer goods—mostly appliances—to war production. Their ads kept their product's name before the public and publicized their role in securing victory. Many advertisements featured consumer products, especially cosmetics, which were tied in some way to women war workers. Others depicted women working for companies that manufactured war goods. This Woodbury Soap advertisement is typical of the effort to tie cosmetics to war work.

She turned her back on the Social Scene and is finding Romance at work!

Her Recipe for Radiance—
a quick Woodbury Facial Cocktail—
does Beauty Duty for
lovely Marguerite Kirchner

SHE'S thrown in her lot for Victory, wiring panel boards for Flying Fortresses in the Boeing Plant, Seattle. Says Marguerite Kirchner: "My job is worth every broken finger nail and dirty oil smudge a million times over!

"Besides," continues Marguerite, "with famous Woodbury Soap to help freshen my complexion, coarse pores and a dingy, dirt-clouded skin are no beauty problems of mine."

Busier lives—but beauty as usual. Keep your complexion clear, smooth. Use Woodbury, the soap made for the *skin* alone. Get it today.

Lovely Marguerite Kirchner of Seattle, Washington, looks trim and feminine in her uniform; says: "The dirt of toil doesn't harm my skin, so long as I take a daily Woodbury Facial Cocktail." Let Woodbury Soap bring loveliness to your skin.

1. **Lunch tastes sweeter** in company of a handsome foreman. Says Marguerite: "I'm in aluminum dust eight hours a day, with no ill effects to my skin. I attribute this to Woodbury."

2. **Time out** for a little relaxation. "I like Woodbury's melting gentleness," Marguerite confesses. Woodbury Facial Soap contains a costly ingredient to insure extra mildness.

3. "**My beauty routine?**" Marguerite explains: "I drench my face in Woodbury's cream-smooth lather. Then scrub till my complexion sparkles, feels fresh again."

4. "**For the Skin You Love to Touch,**" take a Facial Cocktail every day with popular Woodbury Soap. Intended solely to cleanse and clear the skin. Get it today. Only 10¢.

* BACK UP YOUR FIGHTING MAN—BUY WAR BONDS AND STAMPS *

5

Norge Household Appliances Advertisement
"Working for Today...Planning for Tomorrow"
1944

This advertisement from Norge—"Working for Today . . . Planning for Tomorrow"—was typical of those from manufacturers who had shifted from consumer goods to defense production. The ad serves to remind the public that it will be able to enjoy the company's future products. But also key to the ad are the two illustrations—one featuring an attractive woman at work in a factory and the other showing the same lovely woman, now a housewife, at work at her Norge stove.

6

Exhibitor's Sales Guide for the Film
Women At Arms
1942

---

*The Office of War Information's network extended beyond the print
media to include radio and films. The OWI worked closely with
movie studios, both in censoring feature films and in encouraging
the production of films that would serve war aims. The following
document extracts are from a promotional guide for the 1942 RKO
production* Women At Arms. *The description of Mary Brown in the
first promotional excerpt fits closely with the OWI's vision of the woman
defense worker. The account of Mrs. Larkin in the second example
represents another pervasive motif of wartime propaganda about
women.*

The Lady with the Torch

Mary Brown is representative of the forty million women in America
who are working for Victory. In "Women At Arms," second of RKO
Radio Pictures new series of "This Is America," you see Mary Brown
showing the way one out of every eight women in America work in
factories and bomber plants, replacing the men who have gone into
service and creating new jobs in order to keep our production rate
high. Mary Brown's husband was in the National Guard when it was
Federalized and when she had word that he was among the prisoners in the Philippines, she decided that she had a definite part to play
in his release. His last letter to her crystallized her decision to help
make the necessary planes. To become an experienced welder takes
training and in this picture you see Mary Brown actually learning to
weld in a New York welding school. When she is ready for her real job
you see her working on planes in a Baltimore bomber plant, where
she learns that sweaters and feminine wiles are taboo and that real,
hard work is her job and the job of every other man and woman in

---

"Exhibitor's Sales Guide: Women At Arms," 1942, Records of the Office of War
Information (RG 208), National Archives, Box 587.

the plant. She learns to work hour-for-hour with the men and she is proud of her uniform of slacks and blouse and her badge of identification. She is proud of the way she is earning money at a job that accomplishes a more important purpose. Her six-year-old son is in first grade and when she picks him up at the school playground and they walk off hand in hand, it with deep feeling that she looks at the planes flying in the sky overhead and recognizes that they are the planes she herself worked on. She vows to keep 'em flying because in that way lies release for her husband and the thousands of other sons and husbands who are fighting for Victory. Mary Brown is but one of the millions of women doing their share in the war effort. In "Women At Arms" you will see how you can do your part with the WAACS or the WAVES, with the Red Cross, AWVS[1] or Civilian Defense. There is something for every woman who wants to help and this picture will answer the question "What Can I Do?"

Housewives Are Women at Arms Too

Every woman has an opportunity to serve and this picture shows how. Take, for instance, Mrs. Larkin, just plain housewife and many million strong. She would like to join the WAACS, or work on a farm or in a factory, but she has two small children and a house to look after. What can she do? In "Women At Arms," you see the answer that representative women of America have given that question. You see Mrs. Larkin's answer — that if she goes right on being a good housewife, she's among the strongest, bravest and most valuable of American's women-at-arms. She's the keeper of the Home, the thing we're all fighting for. You see the things she can do to help the war effort. You follow her to the hospital where she takes the Red Cross Home Nursing Course or Nutrition Course so that she can keep her family healthy without over-taxing her family doctor. Aside from her duty to her family, Mrs. Larkin shoulders her responsibility as a member of the community. She joins her husband in the OCD[2] and learns how to assist her neighbors in protecting their homes. In "Women At Arms" Mrs. Larkin perhaps can help you to answer the important question "What can I do to help?"

[1]American Women's Voluntary Service.
[2]Office of Civilian Defense.

7

ANNA M. ROSENBERG

Womanpower and the War

April 1943

The Office of War Information and the War Manpower Commission largely ignored African American women in their propaganda efforts, perhaps because of an awareness of resistance to hiring black women. These agencies may have assumed that black women, unlike white women, would not need to be encouraged to enter the labor force. Nonetheless, African American print media received OWI material, and magazines like the Urban League's Opportunity, *the NAACP's* Crisis, *and* Negro Story *publicized war work opportunities for black women.* Opportunity *devoted its entire issue in April 1943 to what it called "Brown Womanpower." The issue led off with the following article by Anna M. Rosenberg of the War Manpower Commission.*

We of the War Manpower Commission have the task of mobilizing and utilizing our nation's manpower and womanpower to the fullest extent. And we are determined to do it in the American way — to guarantee equal rights to work to every man and woman who wants to work.

Your government has decreed that discrimination must go. And I know it is going! Every week more workers and employers realize that the fighters on the Solomons[1] do not ask the creed or color of the men and women who make their guns. Sometimes it may seem to us that the battle against discrimination, like the battle against the Japanese, is a long, slow struggle. Entrenched stupidity and prejudice can be as tenacious as any foe. But you know, and I know, that victory is sometimes slow. As you advance you must fortify and solidify your gains. Only so will the defeat of discrimination be lasting.

The theme of the Eleventh Vocational Opportunity Campaign of the National Urban League is most appropriate — *Womanpower is Vital to Victory.* For without the help of America's women — all its women — we cannot hope to meet our industrial and agricultural labor needs. . . .

More and more employers are making plans to integrate larger numbers of women into their labor force. But this hiring of women will

---

[1]Solomon Islands in the Pacific Ocean.

Anna M. Rosenberg, "Womanpower and the War," *Opportunity*, April 1943, 35–36.

not be uniform. It will vary by industries and areas. The degree of male labor shortage, the nature of the jobs available, and employers' attitudes will influence the extent of the hiring of women.

Probably the largest demands for womanpower will be made by the ordnance and aircraft industries. In 1943 the ordnance industry will require an estimated 500,000 additional workers, while the aircraft industry is expected to take on 650,000 new workers. Over 20 percent of ordnance workers are already women, and before the end of this year there will be more women working in the aircraft industry than there are men.

In other war industries, notably iron and steel and shipbuilding, the use of women is limited by the heavy nature of the work. Job analyses have indicated, however, that considerably more women can be used. The Navy Department, in particular, has encouraged the use of women in government navy yards.

One of the greatest needs for women workers this year will be on farms. By the end of 1943 one agricultural worker out of every ten should be a woman farmer. Negro women can be extensively used on this work. They are familiar with rural conditions, especially in the South. We look to these women to do much to relieve the shortage of farm labor, especially in the harvesting season. For migratory farm labor will be at a premium this year. The men who formerly did that work are in the armed forces, or in war plants. Much of the burden of raising the food to feed wartime America, its fighters, and its allies, rests upon Negro women.

Women are available for all the needs of both industry and agriculture. And they can do the work. The task is to convince employers and male workers of the urgent need to use female workers—both white and colored. And also to convince women that their employment is essential to winning the war.

I realize that Negro womanpower is still largely untapped. Negro women have been the last of the last to be drawn into war production. Only at this date do we find evidence of a growing willingness to accept them. But remember, there was the same difficulty in persuading employers to accept any women workers.

Women can help to meet that difficulty by taking advantage of the training facilities which are now offered in almost every American city. The courses are free and under government supervision. Most of them run from six to eight weeks. Trainees may be able to take night classes without giving up their regular employment. That's hard, I know—but it will help win your fight, and help win America's fight.

I urge Negro women to get all the vocational counseling and schooling that is available. That knowledge will be your best weapon in solidifying our gains both at home and on the battlefront.

2

The Words and Worlds of Women Defense Workers

The civilian women workers of World War II were a diverse group, whose experiences reflected their regional locations, education, race, ethnicity, class, age, and family status. This chapter focuses on defense manufacturing workers as well as private sector employees, while the stories of union activists appear in Chapter 3. Defense manufacturing entailed more than riveting. Women performed an array of tasks, from unskilled labor to jobs that required training and skills. As you read these documents, consider the ways in which these women's experiences were different and how they were similar. What insights do the women offer about the pleasures and challenges of their new jobs?

The first five documents are from oral histories. As with any source, oral histories raised methodological questions. Does selective or poor memory shape these women's stories? Is there any evidence that they are recounting their narratives in ways that reflect the influence of the civil rights or feminist movements that emerged many years after their war work?

8

MATILDA FOSTER

Oral History Account of Shipyard Work

2005

Matilda Foster, a poor black woman originally from rural Arkansas, relocated to Richmond, California, in the San Francisco Bay Area as one of many African Americans who moved to the North and West in the Second Great Migration (see the introduction). Foster first travelled to Missouri, but letters from friends telling about the good wages in California prompted her to move to Richmond, where she worked at a variety of jobs at the Kaiser shipyard. She remained in Richmond the rest of her life and after the war was active in the local NAACP branch. This 2005 interview was conducted by David Washburn and Tiffany Lok of the Rosie the Riveter World War II American Homefront Oral History Project when Foster was eighty-nine.

Foster: Lots of people in my home left and went to St. Louis, Chicago, different places like that. New Jersey. So that's where I went. I liked Missouri, St. Louis, Missouri. A big city, you know.

Washburn: Describe why people were doing that. . . .

Foster: Well, it was a way you could make more money, you know. Better wages, that's why so many people left and emigrated to California because of the money, the better conditions and everything. When so many people had left my home and come to Richmond, California for work. And they'd write and tell us back how much better it was, you know. Us, in Arkansas, once the farm work was over, you didn't have anything to do but fish and hunt or do something like that. Of course you didn't have no job. I did housework, like that, but other than that, where we lived out in the country, it was just you didn't have anything to do, like making a living or whatnot. . . .

As people got older, they were saying kind of wish they had more money they could make. Well, they left. Some had crops, they just left the crops and went on to California. Some of the landlords and things

---

Matilda Foster, interviewed by David Washburn and Tiffany Lok, 2005, Rosie the Riveter World War II American Homefront Oral History Project, Regional Oral History Office, The Bancroft Library, University of California, Berkeley, 2007, 4–5, 8–11, 13–15, 18–19, 21.

that people work for, tried their best to stop folks, you know, from coming and leaving. . . .

I came here, you know, I started working shipyard rate, I started at eighty-eight cents an hours. That was much more than I was making in St. Louis. It was paying sixty cent an hour, that work on factory. I worked at cleaning and pressing shop, ten dollars a day—no, ten dollars a week. . . .

Washburn: Did you move by yourself to St. Louis? Did you live with your sister? What happened?

Foster: I got a room in the same building where my cousin was living, private room, you know. The lady they were renting from, she was the same lady, she had a big flat, you know? So, I was able to get a room there. And I stayed there until I left to come here. [pause]

I came here. One of my sister's father-in-law, he had one of them Harbor-gate houses. There was two apartments, flats, you know? Real nice. Some of them had two and three bedrooms. So I got a room rent from them. . . .

[She then discusses letters that encouraged people to come to California.]

Washburn: When you are talking about living conditions, did any of those letters, when they were talking about living conditions mention anything about Jim Crow,[1] and out here there not being segregation?

Foster: Yeah, yeah! Some people [sure did make much about how in this state?] it wasn't segregation and things. You could go and sit down in the restaurant and eat anywhere you wanted to out here. But you couldn't do that at my home. In a white man's restaurant, no, you couldn't just go in any of them and have food. Some would take you and some wouldn't. . . .

Washburn: Now, people say actually, about Richmond that Richmond was that way in some ways too.

Foster: That's what they say, yeah.

Washburn: Did you see that as well?

Foster: No.

Washburn: I mean there weren't signs up but it was kind of like, you knew.

Foster: It was one place on MacDonald, now, since you asked me, they said they didn't take colored in there for eating. I forgot what the name of it was but I never went there. I liked a place on 6th and MacDonald, they used to have a little restaurant there. I forget what they called it, but they had some of the best roast beef you want to eat.

[1]The term *Jim Crow* referred to segregation of the races.

And they was owned by white people. And the lady, I would order roast beef so much and apple pie and ice cream and stuff like that, she got where she knew me. When I come in, she ask me "What's your dish today, roast beef?" [laughter] . . .

[Foster discusses the process of moving to California.]

Washburn: I'm trying to think, was that something that in people's letters, they wrote back? And was that something you, yourself, were looking forward to? That the whole institution of segregation wasn't going to be in California? Was that something that you were conscious about?

Foster: No, I wasn't worried too much about the segregation. The thing I was looking forward most to was making more money right then and a better place to live in.

Because it was funny when you come to California, you could hear black folks calling white people by their name. Because the young girls were "Missy" girls, back in the South, you had to "Miss" them, you know. It was an insult to the parents if you called them by their name. The thing that shows you how different states and things are. . . .

[The interviewer asks about her job.]

Foster: I started out working in the [short?] yard, they called it "the yard." Working and picking up and cleaning the streets and things like that. And then the next couple of months, they told me it would pay more scaling.[2] And I took a test to get that job. They paying a $1.45 an hour. From the bottom we had to climb — and you know how tall the ships are — we had to climb the ship ladder from the bottom to the top, then we get to the top, and had to go back down to the bottom, all the way down to the bottom of the ship. That got a little too rough for me. I did a couple of months, then I took sick went to the hospital. The doctor recommended [I be took out of double bottom?][3] That was in the scaling department. And that paid $1.05 per hour. Then after I got well, went back, they put me on [the offset?] dock. And that was paying a $1.00 per hour. And so, I worked there until shipyard was laid off. They began layoffs in '45. I got laid off in May. . . .

---

[2]"Mill scale" is a residue of brittle iron oxide on steel, so Foster is referring to removing the scale with a knife.

[3]"Double-bottom" refers to a ship with a two-layered hull.

built one, but they had not built it according to the blueprints; they had made improvements. So my job was to correct and get those up to date to what they had already done. I spent—I don't know if it really was months, but it seemed like months. . . .

We had senior draftsmen; they were actually in another room. They did the beautiful, beautiful drawings. We just helped relieve them from doing this little stuff that needed to be done. It was important work, but it was time-consuming and they really had more important things to do. But they never treated us with any disrespect. Never got the feeling of it. We were just a group of teenaged kids. I actually went to work when I was seventeen and they didn't realize that, so I had to get square with the Social Security people later on. A lot of people— military guys fibbed about their age too, to get into the service. There was a lot of that and I guess maybe they just looked the other way because we wanted to help. We wanted to do our bit to bring the war to the end. Our country was fighting on both sides, in Europe and in the South Pacific. It was a time of great patriotism, I mean really great. . . .

[Sousa discusses her mother's decision to work as well.]

When I said the family came down, eventually my dad got transferred to Camp Stoneman which is out here by Pittsburg. So the rest of the family came down into my sister's little house, briefly before they all moved out. But during that time, my mother decided she wanted to do something, too. Her three daughters were already working and she decided she wanted to, so someone told her if she joined the Painters Union, it was a good job. She had a difficult time. First of all, she was already a grandmother and she was a woman. They didn't want women in the unions. My two sisters had a very difficult time getting in the unions. They were early people. My mother did, too. It took her three tries at this hiring hall. The first time she showed up like ladies did in the '40s with her hat and her gloves and her trim little suit. Well, working on the shipyards— [laughs] so the third time she showed up with a bandana around her head and my brother's jean jacket on, shoved her hands in her pockets and said she wanted a job. She got hired. . . . She was a taper, and she would tape off the areas they didn't want painted, like the brass plates and that stuff. She was always on her hands and knees taping off areas. . . . Actually, she worked longer than the rest of us. When I was pregnant, then I worked a full year and then I quit; then my sister Margie got married and then she got pregnant and then she quit; then my sister Phyllis, she was married, but her husband had an asthma problem around here, so they went to Texas. She actually worked at Todd Houston shipyards in Texas, which was a different experience and I hope that you get to interview her, because my sister has stories to tell. She really typifies a Rosie. . . .

[Stine asks Sousa about the people she worked with.]

Sousa: Actually, I tried to keep my high school friends, and I've since lost track. But people were from all over, and in fact in our community we didn't have any black people. So it was kind of a revelation to see all the black people. I imagine it was the same for them. People were still segregated when this all happened. At the shipyards, they were not segregated. You had crews that had everybody of every color. One of the ladies said that she was sitting there, eating lunch, and this black man sitting by her said, "This would have never happened in the South," that he could sit there and they were joking around and stuff. It was a different atmosphere, which is probably hard for you to even imagine. They had some hard times, because it was hard for them to join the union. In fact, my sister Phyllis was told when she applied, "We don't take women and we don't take blacks." That was it. That was the Boilermakers. They did, but I understand they had a separate union for black people, which is dumb. If people can do the same work, they should get the same wages and the same privileges and pay the same dues. [laughs] If you're going to pay the same dues, you should have an equal everything. I don't remember any problems, racial-wise. I don't remember anything at all, but you've got to remember I was only 17 or 18 years old and sometimes your head is in the clouds. Newly married, and things were different. I suppose older people saw things differently than I did, but I was really young at the time. It was an exciting time. . . .

[Stine later asks about who took care of her sister's child when Sousa went to work.]

Sousa: When I left, there were other people there that could help with the babysitting but eventually when everybody got their own places, she had another family living with her that had a child the same age as her son. They were very grateful to have a place to live. . . . But child-care, Kaiser developed their own system in the child development centers, which went—some of them—day and night because of the shifts. They were always packed. My younger sister, for a while, was in childcare. She was a little older, she wasn't a baby. She was seven or something like that. . . .

Stine: I know that things must have really changed a lot when the end of the war came. There were all these new people here, and all these jobs that had been defense jobs were all of a sudden no longer. You were no longer working in the shipyards *[she quit when she had her first baby]*, but I wonder if you had a sense of people planning and knowing that there would be an inevitable end, or if it was just kind of the rug pulled out from underneath people?

Sousa: I think it was the rug pulled out from under people. Not only women, but all of the industries that Richmond was known for—I mean, we had four shipyards going here. Of course, the women were laid off first so that the men could come back and take those jobs, but there wasn't a need to build ships anymore. So a lot of unemployment—my husband was lucky enough to have a skill, he was a carpenter. He got a job right away when he came out of the service, so we weren't affected, but a lot of people were. It took a while. I wasn't involved in government, or how the city ran. I'm still the mindset [as?] a homemaker, so a lot of this stuff didn't involve me or I wasn't involved with it, so I couldn't answer some of your questions. . . .

[After Sousa's children were older, she returned to work as a school bus driver for special needs children.]

Stine: At the end of the war, you felt like things were, at least for you, going back to maybe how they would've been before.

Sousa: Yes, that's what we expected. None of us ever expected to have a career. The guys signed up for a hitch in the service, and that's what we did. We signed up for a time when our country needed us, just like the guys did. We went back to what we did before, and that's what we expected. Although there were women who needed to keep their jobs, there were a lot that needed to do that, older people supporting kids. When you think of people who came from the South, especially black women that were supporting children, they needed to keep their jobs. That's the way it was. . . .

[Sousa returns to discussing her mother's work experience.]

Stine: When your mom came down to work, did you get the sense that she really did this out of a sense of obligation or a sense of patriotism or duty, rather than necessarily needing to have the paycheck? Or was it a combination?

Sousa: It was a combination. She was part of the Veterans of Foreign Wars Auxiliary and she was very patriotic. The fact that my father had passed away by then, she needed to have a job, too. It's a combination of everything, but the fact that she could do it—she said she was very, very, very proud of the fact that she only got spray-painted once. [laughs] So she knew you had to keep so far ahead of that gang. If you lagged behind then you got sprayed.

10

MAGGIE GEE

Oral History Account of Work at Shipyards and of Being a WASP

2003

Maggie Gee, a Chinese American woman from Berkeley, California, had two different war jobs. Right out of high school, much like Marian Sousa, she became a draftsman for a shipbuilding company. She used her wages to take private flying lessons and eventually became a pilot in the Women's Airforce Service Pilots (WASP). Gee discusses the Chinese American community she was part of, as well as the discrimination Chinese Americans encountered. Her Chinese American mother, for example, who was born in the United States and thus a citizen, married an immigrant from China. In 1922 the federal Cable Act decreed that female citizens who married men ineligible for citizenship (which in effect meant Asian immigrants who were legally barred from naturalization) lost their own citizenship, and thus Gee's mother became a noncitizen at the age of twenty-seven. But in this excerpt from her oral history, Maggie Gee focuses on the employment opportunities World War II offered both her and her mother. Widowed during the Great Depression, Gee's mother took in sewing and cleaned houses, and quickly took advantage of the opportunity to work as a steel burner (cutter) in the shipyards. Maggie Gee was a student at the University of California, which offered a training program that led to her defense job. Leah McGarrigle, Robin Li, and Kathryn Stine conducted the oral history interview in 2003 when Maggie Gee was eighty years old.

Maggie Gee, interviewed by Leah McGarrigle, Robin Li, and Kathryn Stine, 2003, Rosie the Riveter World War II American Homefront Oral History Project, Regional Oral History Office, The Bancroft Library, University of California, Berkeley, 22–23, 48–50, 65–66.

Li: How did your mother transition from housework to defense work?

Gee: You know, it's really surprising, though. I wish I knew. She realized, I guess, that there was need, and she started very early, I think when the war first started, to apply for a job out in the shipyards. It was a real job. I think that was the important thing. It was a real job and you did something for the war effort. Someone else must have told her, but she might have found out all by herself, because I don't think any of her friends went out to work in the shipyards. Maybe there was a group of younger generations, but I don't remember, though. Someone might have said, you know, there's good jobs out in the shipyards and you could do something for the war effort and make good money. She really enjoyed that. My sister was telling us. I guess I wasn't at home at that particular time, but she really enjoyed getting up in the morning, going to work, and feeling as if she were doing something and being out there with other people. . . .

Li: Do you think that your mother felt conflicted, because she had lost her citizenship earlier?

Gee: She might have felt that this is one way of proving it, too. She did. You could work in the shipyards and not be a citizen. You could join the Army and not be a citizen. . . .

[Gee explains how she got her drafting job.]

U.C. had this program to train you if you wanted to become a draftsman, if you had trigonometry. You had to have a little bit of mathematics. If you had a little bit of trigonometry or you knew how to draw a line, or you had the concept of what a ship looks like, how to draw things. . . . I must have read something in the Daily Cal and decided to go for this training and get this job. It was really more direct; one felt that it was more directly involved in the war effort. It was the war effort. You wanted to get involved in the war effort.

Stine: How long of a course was that?

Gee: It was all day, and it might have been six, or eight, or ten weeks. I'm not sure, now. It was just training to work as a draftsman. You're working as a draftsman, you're working with an engineer, and he needs some drawings. You have to understand a little bit of what you were drawing, though. You were an assistant to him. You started out as an assistant to an engineer. I was pretty good at that, because I was mathematically inclined and I knew I could understand a lot of things that an engineer might understand, just as a lay person, so it didn't baffle me at all. . . .

[Stein asks her about her ambition to be a pilot and to fly with the WASP.]

Gee: It was sort of a dream; it's not an ambition, it's a dream that one has. Because of the war, I could earn a little bit of money to learn to fly. But it was being in the service that gave me the opportunity to do all the flying that I wanted to do, large planes. . . .

Stine: How did you seek out the opportunity to get involved with the armed forces and flying? How did that happen, that transition from Mare Island to flying? How did you make that choice?. . .

Gee: There were three women, three girls, and we were looking for something else to do that was joining one of the services, but we were too young. . . . But I went to learn to fly on my own, because I had enough money to buy the flying time. I went up to Minden, Nevada to learn to fly. The recruiters for the WASPs at that particular time were coming through Reno, Nevada, so at that time I got interviewed. I passed all the examinations and qualifications, and I was accepted. There were twenty-five thousand women that applied, and I felt very fortunate. About two or three thousand of us were accepted, and then half of us washed out of training. I didn't wash out of training, I was lucky to finish.

[Gee served with the WASP for a year until it was disbanded in 1945.]

11

MARGARITA SALAZAR McSWEYN

Oral History Account of Work at a Lockheed Plant
1980

Margarita Salazar McSweyn was sixty-four when her interview took place in 1980. Interviewer Sherna Gluck compiled a streamlined transcript, a portion of which appears here. McSweyn's family, which identified as Hispanic, moved from New Mexico to Los Angeles when McSweyn was a child. She was raised mostly speaking Spanish and started working in a factory in order to finance her beauty school training. She was working for a friend, Molly, as a beautician when the war began. She was twenty-five when she started work at Lockheed as a driller. Although surveys indicated that the majority of women in defense work wanted to keep their jobs after the war ended, McSweyn had

Sherna Berger Gluck, *Rosie the Riveter Revisited: Women, the War, and Social Change* (New York: New American Library, 1987), 85–97.

different aspirations and eventually became a bookkeeper. Although she took some time out for childrearing, she worked most of her adult life.

I quit Molly [beauty shop operator] and went to work for defense. I could make more money. I could see that I wasn't going to make that much money working as an operator and the money was in defense. Everybody would talk about the overtime and how much more money it was. And it was exciting. Being involved in that era you figure you were doing something for your country—and at the same time making money.

There was ads all over. I thought I would give it a try and see if I could do it. There was so much talk about it being such hard work, and I had never done hard work. The ads, they'd talk about the riveting and running some sort of machine—dimpling, I think they called it. It wasn't for the glamour. You weren't going to meet all these guys; you would be working primarily with women.

My girlfriends used to tell me, "Why are you going to try that when you have this nice, clean job here?" I thought it'd be a whole new experience. Find out if it was as lucrative as they said. And then being that my brothers would talk about going in the navy, I guess I felt it was something new, why not try it. I knew I could always come back to what I was doing as long as I kept my operator's license.

They checked you out, your American citizenship and stuff like that. They told you what to wear: pants and a hair net, always. Makeup, they didn't care, as long as you wore your pants and wore sensible shoes and kept your hair out of the way.

That first day, when I went, I was startled. That building is pretty large and each floor had something different. I think there were six or seven floors. It was so huge, I used to get lost going from one department to another, till finally I got to know the other girls and I'd go in and out with them. . . .

[McSweyn's work was initially drilling on airplane wings.]

I don't think I found [the work] so hard or that it made such a big impression on me to say that oh, my arm was breaking off. If I was willing to work overtime, it must have been possible. I did the same thing for about a year: drilling, drilling, always drill work.

In our crew of twenty or thirty, there were about four men. They would put the wing in its proper place so you could work on it—moving things and doing the heavier work. There were some older women we assumed were married. There were other Mexican women, but I don't recall too many colored girls, not in our little section there. But when we'd go to lunch, I'd see a lot of them. We all blended in—men, women, Mexican, Italian. . . .

I started complaining about my legs, but you didn't change jobs just because you had a whim. You really had to have a reason, especially if you were a good steady employee that they could depend on to work overtime. I had gone to the doctor and gotten shots for my legs, for veins, so I actually had a good reason. Still, it took a while. I had to go through an interview with a lady there and express myself why and bring in my proofs.

I wanted to work sitting down. They asked me if I would like to do office work. . . . They figured that the toolshed would be the best, because I wouldn't have to walk so much. I'd help the man that was in charge. There was just the two of us there. It was hectic when they'd come in with bunches that wanted tools, but it was much easier for me. And cleaner because just your hands got dirty, nothing else. And you didn't have to wear a hair net. You'd just dress in pants.

But after I started working there at the toolshed, I kept thinking of getting out of there. . . .

[She went to work for a beauty company.]

I started as a desk girl. I know that I took less money, but I always admired beauty work. I was trained for it and it was more my type of thing. I got to dress up entirely different, working more with women. Also, I figured, the war was just about over. Make your break now before all the girls will be looking for jobs. And it was a good chance. At Lockheed I saw where I was going to stay, whereas over here I had a chance of good opportunities to advance. But I think in a way the job at Lockheed did have an impact because I got to know about tools, which I never did before. I could clean something or go back there in cracks and drill a hole. Not that I'm mechanically inclined, but I was able to do it. . . .

[She became a telephone operator and receptionist for the company and took bookkeeping at night to improve her opportunities with the company.]

I was taking one day at a time. I knew I wanted to get married. But I wasn't positive as to the role I would accept afterward, whether I would keep on working or whether he [Alex, her fiancé, who was in the military] would come back and we'd get settled or what tomorrow would bring. It was such an upheaval that I didn't know.

[McSweyn worked after she got married until her first pregnancy. Eventually she returned to part-time work as a bookkeeper to help pay for the children's Catholic school education. When the interviewer asked her if she would have changed anything, she said that "she might make other choices if she were a young woman starting out today."]

12

FAITH TRAVERSIE

Oral History Account of Shipyard Work
2005

Faith Traversie, a Lakota originally from South Dakota, moved to Vallejo, California, to be a welder after her sister, who lived there, told her of the job opportunities at the Mare Island shipyard. Traversie had three children, two of whom she left with relatives and an infant whom she took with her to California. Her husband was in the navy and served abroad. Like many other Native Americans of her generation, she was educated at an Indian boarding school. Her oral history has a rich discussion of the welding work she did on heavy cruisers in the shipyards and the pleasure she took in her ability. In part of her interview, she discusses the experiences of Native Americans in the shipyard. She was interviewed by Elizabeth Castle for the Rosie the Riveter Project in 2005.

Castle: I read a little story where it said there wasn't an option for you to check, to say that you were American Indian, so you put down "Other"?

Traversie: Oh! Yes! [laughs] That was an incident with me. Yeah. They had all the two rows on a big page, regular sized sheet paper, two long rows named every nationality you could think of! But Native American it didn't. It had other on the bottom, so I check other.

So, [laughs] I handed my paper in, and oh my God! This Navy officer said, "Sit down a minute. Sit there on the chair." So, he goes and calls another guy, another officer, so they read it! "Oh my God!" Whatever they—then, they called the third guy, they finally had to go up to, mind you, the captain, the *highest* on the base. [laughs] How to rate me!? Here they had to name me, and name me as an American citizen. Let's see, were we rated as white?

And then of course, it had American Indian, you know, Native American Indian. But, no, they had to—they couldn't say Native American because see, there are Native Americans over here, that were born here and they claim to be natives, see. Native Americans.

Faith Traversie, interviewed by Elizabeth Castle, 2005, Rosie the Riveter World War II American Homefront Oral History Project, Regional Oral History Office, The Bancroft Library, University of California, Berkeley, 11–12.

Castle: So that word wasn't used to describe Indian people.

Traversie: Uh-uh. So, they called us American Indian, I guess, Native American Indian. . . . But they finally got it straightened out.

Castle: Were there other Indian people working?

Traversie: Oh yeah, oh yeah. All Oklahoma, there were a lot of people from the South, all over.

Castle: Really? In the shipyards?

Traversie: In fact, I welded with an Oklahoma Indian girl, young woman. She wasn't married yet and she was a welder from—but we all had to go to welding school because such jobs weren't open to women before the war, so—

Castle: Right, so you had to get the training.

Traversie: So, I think that they treated women fairly, I thought we were treated fairly.

Castle: And you were saying, when I first started to ask you the question, that you didn't experience a lot of prejudice or racism.

Traversie: No. I never did. Because there was every kind of— [laughs]—you know? Some of foreign descent. [cross talk] . . .

[In reference to the many races at the yard, she recounts an incident.]

We were doing our welding and here, there were some men *gathering*. [in hushed suspenseful tones] They were on board the ship working, too, and pretty soon *all* of them were gathering over there. And they were looking at me! I was welding on a gun turret down on the floor of the ship, the main deck, I mean, welding on this gun turret. And I looked and those men were all looking at me and I thought, "I wonder what—? Is it the job? Wonder what they're planning?" I wondered why! But I snapped down my hood again and I was welding again. And pretty soon I start getting my gear together, and my watchman, he was right beside me and he was helping gather up my gear. And here, this man came over. He was a Navy man and here he came over, and he said, "Lady, I'd like to ask you a personal question, would you mind?" I said, "Well no. What is it? Go ahead," you know. He said, "Well, you know, we're having a big argument up there, that group of men," he said, "They are trying to decide what nationality you are," because I spoke such good English, see, I had no language accent. He said, "You speak such good English. In fact, you speak better English than some of our other workers." [laughter] . . . "Well, I'm an American Indian," I said, "I'm a Sioux Indian from South Dakota. I belong to the Yankton? [*sic*] Sioux tribe." [shouts] . . . He took off! He said, "You're all wrong! You're all wrong!" [uproarious laughter] . . .

Traversie: Yeah. They said, "We thought you were Mexican, but there's no way. She don't talk or act like a Mexican." Then they thought I was Oriental. They thought I was either some kind of like, Chinese or Hawaiian or—they had me Hawaiian for a while. . . . They were all wrong. They never guessed American Indian. . . .

[Castle asks whether there were any Indian organizations that had social gatherings.]

Traversie: Oh, they [had] Indian organizations *all over* the West Coast. Indian—I was going to say clubs, but Indian organizations. They had, but gee, you were so busy working, you were working during the war at that time. . . . *[She explains that there were many organizations because]* they shipped a *lot* of Indian people in to work because they came in experienced, you know. They had schooling. A *lot* of them, they had schooling in different trades. So they were just *grabbed* up like that, American Indians, yeah.

Castle: Why would you say they had the trade schooling? Did that come from boarding school?

Traversie: Boarding school, yeah! Back from the reservations. . . .

Castle: So that was a trade that mostly men probably could take in boarding schools.

Traversie: Yeah, uh, huh.

Castle: Whereas women had certain other options.

Traversie: But mostly it was wartime welding.

13

POLLY CROW

A Defense Worker's Letters to Her Husband

June 12, 1944, and January 30, 1945

Polly Crow's letters to her husband, William, who was away in the military, offer valuable insights into the problems of a working mother.

Judy Barrett Litoff and David C. Smith, *Since You Went Away: World War II Letters from American Women on the Home Front* (Lawrence: University Press of Kansas, 1991), 147, 150.

Crow had worked as a bookkeeper before her marriage and the birth of her son, Bill. With her husband in the army, she moved to Louisville, Kentucky, to live with her mother. In her letters to William, she explained that she wanted a job to save money for his return and gave accounts of her work as a bookkeeper for a machine company engaged in defense work. Polly took a similar job working for a telephone company after the war.

June 12, 1944

Darlin':

You are now the husband of a career woman — just call me your little Ship Yard Babe! Yeh! I made up my mind that I wanted to work from 4:00 p.m. 'till midnight so's I could have my cake and eat it too. I wanted to work but didn't want to leave Bill all day — in the first place it would be too much for Mother altho' she was perfectly willing, and then Bill needs me. This way Mother will just have to feed him once and tuck him in which is no trouble at all any more as I just put him in bed and let him play quietly until he's ready to go to sleep and he drops right off. . . . I finally ended up with just want I wanted. Comptometer[1] [calculator] job — 4:00 'till midnight — 70 cents an hour to start which amounts to $36.40 a week, $145.60 per month, increase in two months if I'm any good and I know I will be. Oh yeh! At Jeffersonville Boat and Machine Co. I'll have to go over to Jeffersonville, Ind. which will take about 45 minutes each way. Hope I can get a ride home each nite as that's the only feature I dislike but I'm not gonna be a sissy. If I can't get a ride, I'll get tags for our buggy and probably use it. . . . If I don't need it for work I may not get them but will just have to see how things work out. Want to take Bill out swimming a lot this summer so I may need it for that. . . .

Opened my little checking account too and it's a grand and a glorious feeling to write a check all your own and not have to ask for one. Any hoo, I don't want it said I charged things to 'em and didn't pay it so we don't owe anybody anything and I'm going to start sockin' it in the savings and checking too so's we'll have something when our sweet little Daddy comes home.

[1]A comptometer, a mathematical device, was a key-driven adding machine.

[Despite her determination to work at night, on occasion Crow was asked to work a day shift.]

Jan. 30, 1945

Darlin':

Thought for a while this a.m. I would have to take Bill to work with me, or stay at home. He was evidently dreaming a bad dream and awakened just as I was getting up. He wanted me and no one else would do and while I ate breakfast, he clung onto me like he'd never let me go. We finally convinced him that I was just going to work until 10:00. Going out into the snow at 7:00 a.m. and catching buses wasn't half bad and I really enjoyed it. I was the only one out on our street, and lots of houses had lights on which looked very welcoming. I liked the feeling of not depending on some one else to get me to and from work. However if I get a regular ride, I'll take it too sometime for it seems like I don't have any time with Bill at all. Got home at 6:00 this afternoon as I had to stop and get the groceries for tomorrow. By the time we ate, did the dishes, I washed out a few things, mended the fur coat again and bathed us both, it was time to go to bed. Bill and I are sitting in bed writing you but he is having a horrible time getting enough stationery, as he has already had three sheets and is yelling for more. Yet, he even scribbled on this [V-Mail] as you can see. He gets a bigger kick out of writing Daddy than anything else he does. I'm going to teach him to say his little prayers for you each nite. Good nite, Darlin'.

I love you forever, Polly

14

LONG BEACH AIRVIEW NEWS

Mother of Seven Builds B-17s; Has Super Attendance Mark

July 13, 1943

Company newspapers can also offer a glimpse of women workers' lives inside and outside of the factory, although admittedly they paint a rosy

"Mother of Seven Builds B-17s; Has Super Attendance Mark," *Long Beach Airview News,* July 13, 1943, 11.

*picture designed to boost morale within the company and promote
commitment to work. For example, some large Southern California
companies like Douglas and Lockheed, faced with a diverse workforce
and severe labor shortages, promoted interracial and inter-ethnic
cooperation by frequently featuring Mexican American and African
American women in their employee magazines. The following article
in the* Long Beach Airview News *showcases Douglas worker Celia
Dominguez. The piece was accompanied by a photograph of Dominguez
at work with her rivet gun and another featuring her seven children
who "beam broadly as they relate how proud" they are of their mother
who builds airplanes. The article offers quotations from Dominguez, but
leaves us wanting to know more about her and the challenges she faced
balancing her responsibilities.*

If ever there was a woman who could legitimately plead excused absence
and frequently clock in late—it's Celia Dominguez, but not she.

According to Leadman Donald Dewitt, . . . Celia has never missed
a day or been late since she came to Douglas eight months ago, as a
framer and skinner on wing leading edges for the B-17. Truth is, Celia
isn't the kind of woman who lets a little problem like seven children
keep her from plane-building for her six nephews in the Armed
Forces.

Mrs. Dominguez is justly proud of her family, which in turn con-
siders it pretty wonderful to have mother helping produce planes at
Douglas. . . .

*[The article describes some of the academic and musical accomplish-
ments of her children and notes that her husband, the Reverend Alphonso
Dominguez, is also musically inclined. He was in charge of two Methodist
churches located in Fullerton and Anaheim.]*

Mrs. Dominguez says, "My husband encourages me to do my part
for our country, and my Fullerton neighbors where we have lived for
12 years, are so kind and helpful that I can gratify my desire to help my
country with a free mind, and do my part to see that my six nephews in
the Armed Forces get the equipment they need."

15

Photograph of Aircraft Workers
1944

Photographs are rich documents of working women's experiences during World War II. Government agencies commissioned thousands of pictures demonstrating the variety of women's jobs as well as the diversity of defense workers. Some photographs focused on individual women as they stood next to large machinery. In keeping with the propaganda agenda of the Office of War Information, the photographed women were often attractive and carefully groomed to reflect the way in which they

Library of Congress, Prints & Photographs Division, Reproduction number LC-USW33-028626-C (b&w film neg.)

*maintained their femininity despite their labor. Other photographs had
a more "candid" quality and showed women at their work. What does
this photograph of two Douglas Aircraft employees convey about their
experiences? The information provided about this image gives some
hint as to what message the photograph was intended to convey: "The
six plane factories of the Douglas Aircraft Company have been termed
an industrial melting pot, since men and women of fifty-eight national
origins worked side by side in pushing America's output. S. O. Porter,
Douglas director of personnel, recently declared that Negros [sic]
are doing an outstanding job in all plants. Dora Miles and Dorothy
Johnson are employed in the Long Beach Plant of the Douglas Aircraft
Company."*

16

MRS. T. H. WOOD

Letter to Eleanor Roosevelt about Racial Discrimination in the Kingsbury Ordnance Plant

July 31, 1942

*Despite the harmony suggested by the photograph in Document 15, racial
tensions for both women and men did permeate defense plants and their
surrounding communities. Faced with discrimination in factory plants,
African Americans sought assistance from federal government officials
and agencies. Many wrote personal letters to the president and first lady.
Mrs. T. H. Wood's complaint against the Kingsbury Ordnance Plant in
Indiana was one of dozens forwarded to the Fair Employment Practices
Commission (FEPC). Although the FEPC had some successes in other
cities, it made little progress in improving circumstances for black workers
at Kingsbury. Wood's letter is signed with two "V's," which was a slogan
African Americans used during the war to refer to victory abroad, but also
victory at home in the fight for civil rights.*

Records of the Committee on Fair Employment Practice, Region VI, Box 67, folder 1,
Record Group 22, National Archives, Chicago.

Mrs. T. H. Wood
Gary, Indiana
July 31, 1942

Dear Mrs. Roosevelt,
    Located within a few miles distance of this vicinity is the following plant:
    Todd and Brown, Inc.
    Kingsbury Ordnance Plant
    La Porte, Indiana.
From information previously received defense work is now being done there.
    In the conflict . . . during World War number I I served my country as I best could by doing governmental work.
    I have attempted recently to receive a position as a matron at the previous mentioned enterprise. This was done without success. From observation it seems as if my color or race (Negro) is the only factor that prevents my receiving this position.
    I volunteered my services at the age of sixteen during the first World War and worked at the Conservatory of Music in Cincinnati Ohio in the upper barracks cafeteria.
    I am physically able to work and I feel entitled to a position in which I can serve my country again. I also have the responsibility of supporting my mother who is seventy-one years of age and refuses to accept a pension because of her belief that the government has enough responsibility already.
    If there is any possible way in which you can aid me, I would appreciate it very much if you would do so immediately.
    Patriotically yours,
    (Mrs.) T. H. Woods
    [signed with two V's]

17

LAURA WASHINGTON CYRUS

Affidavit Regarding Racial Discrimination

June 5, 1942

In contrast to Mrs. Woods's handwritten and informal letter to Eleanor Roosevelt, Laura Washington Cyrus, adopted daughter of prominent black leader Booker T. Washington, swore out an affidavit detailing her complaints about racial discrimination at the Kingsbury plant. She submitted a second affidavit from one of her supervisors, Miss Patricia Pensinger, a white woman, which confirmed Cyrus's competency. The Fair Employment Practices Commission forwarded the complaint to the company, which responded by saying that her work had been satisfactory for the first two weeks but that subsequently "you assumed duties and authority beyond the call of your assignment and to the extent of signing as a forelady in the forelady's absence, to the dissatisfaction of your immediate superior, Mrs. Mary Burton." She was not reinstated.

MRS. LAURA WASHINGTON CYRUS, being first duly sworn upon her oath says:

That she presently resides at 332½ East Michigan Street, Michigan City, Indiana; that she is a graduate of Tuskegee Institute and the adopted daughter of the late Booker T. Washington; that on the 5th day of April, 1942 she was employed by the Kingsbury Ordnance Plant of Laporte, Indiana as a detonator line operator; that on the 3rd day of May, 1942, her services were terminated at said plant for the reason that "Her Services unsatisfactory."

That this affiant feel that she has been discriminated against in the matter of reasons given for her discharge because she is a colored girl and in support of said discriminatory charge advances the following facts, to-wit: that within two weeks after her employment as a line operator she was transferred from said position of line operator to that of sub-forelady which latter position she kept until the day of her discharge; that in her capacity as sub-forelady she interviewed in excess

Records of the Committee on Fair Employment Practices, Region VI, Box 67, folder 1, Record Group 22, National Archives, Chicago.

of three hundred prospective operators and none of her selectees were rejected by her superiors, Mrs. Mary Burton and Miss Patricia Pensinger; that for the six weeks immediately preceding her discharge she was working in the office of her department as a personnel worker, interviewing colored line operators, training them, giving safety talks, making out package and locker passes, First Aid cards and during a two week illness of Mrs. Mary Burton ran this office with Miss Patricia Pensinger; that on several occasions the work of this affiant was praised by Mrs. Burton and a Mrs. Buman; this affiant further states that on May 27th one Mr. Wellman, assistant to a Mr. Barenzelli, line foreman, came into a training class being conducted by this affiant and loudly called her by her first name which fact this affiant resented in the presence of those whose successful training to a great degree depended upon the amount of respect accorded her by her superiors; that the said Mr. Wellman always referred to Mrs. Burton and Miss Pensinger by their proper titles and this affiant had previously explained the importance of this to Mrs. Burton; that this affiant thereafter spoke to Mr. Barenzelli about this incident with Mrs. Wellman, whereupon the said Mr. Barenzelli informed this affiant that he was not interested in personalities and was only interested in how much work was produced; affiant further states that although she was actually performing all the duties of a forelady she was paid the rate of a line operator as are all colored "Bay foreladies" the term given colored women who actually do the supervision of the line operators but are paid 60c per hour while less experienced white girls are brought over to these colored lines and given the title forelady at 75¢ per hour; that all of the operators on the lines in the department in which this affiant worked were colored; affiant further states that at no time prior to her discharge on June 3, 1942 was she informed of any dissatisfaction with her work and that in view of the further fact that out of eight weeks employment six of them were occupied with work of a supervisory character and of a much more responsible character the termination of her employment because of unsatisfactory service is highly unjust, illogical and only attributable to her insistence upon being accorded the same amount of respect in the presence of those of whom she had been placed in charge.

Affiant, therefore, prays the proper authorities of the Kingsbury Ordnance Plant to correct this injustice by espunging [sic] from her termination slip that portion of same referring to her unsatisfactory services and to reinstate her to her proper status as an employee and failing in this affiant prays the War Production Board to investigate the facts herein with a view toward the bettering of working conditions among colored employees of said plant and thereby increasing efficiency of their work in the vital war effort of America.

3

Union Women

During the war women's participation in unions increased, as did their opportunities for leadership roles as male leaders left for the military. Women in the United Electrical, Radio and Machine Workers of America (UE) and the United Automobile, Aircraft and Agricultural Implement Workers of America (UAW) are particularly well documented. In the electrical industry, women constituted a significant proportion of the workforce before the war (32.2 percent in 1940), and the UE was relatively quick to take up the call for fair treatment of women war workers. In contrast, the auto industry employed only 5.7 percent in 1940. UAW members initially were hostile to the encroachment of women on their turf, but the UAW eventually actively sought to recruit women union members and was willing to address issues of concern to women workers. The documents that follow highlight women's union activism during the war. What were the key issues for women workers? What particular concerns did African American union women have?

18

UNITED ELECTRICAL, RADIO AND MACHINE WORKERS OF AMERICA

Minutes of the "Women to Win the War Conference"
December 13, 1942

The December 1942 conference "Women to Win the War," which was held for Ohio women of the United Electrical, Radio and Machine

United Electrical, Radio and Machine Workers of America, District Council No. 7, "Minutes of the 'Women to Win the War Conference,'" December 13, 1942, 8–11, Women's Bureau, Record Group 86, Box 865, National Archives, Washington, D.C.

*Workers of America (UE), reflects the UE's relatively enlightened
stance on women. The conference reviewed the successes the UE had
already made in negotiating equal pay for equal work in contracts
and acknowledged the efforts of individual women. It also featured
several guest speakers. One was Elizabeth Christman of the U.S.
Women's Bureau, whose presence underlined the way in which the
Bureau sought to encourage women union leaders during the war.
A second speaker was Bessie Kemp, a black UE woman leader from
New Jersey, whose comments speak to the UE's progressive stance on
racial discrimination.*

Elizabeth Christman

The evil system of one job rate for women—because they are
women—must be rooted out of our industrial life. It is contrary to the
fundamental principles of trade unionism, and a danger to both men
and women wage earners.

One of the favorite ways to try to justify lower wages for women
workers is to say, "A woman never does a man's work. The company
must hire a helper or install special machinery for heavy lifting or carrying." Or, "It isn't the same job that the man did. He had more all-
around skills. They broke down the job so that it is no longer skilled
work."

Train a woman properly, put her on a job, and she will be able to
do a man's work—the part of the job that requires brain power and
coordinated muscles. Why should the energies of a machine operator,
a man or woman, be dissipated by heavy lifting or hauling, work which
can be done satisfactorily by helpers or mechanized devices? The con-
served energy of the machine operator will be used where it should
be—to increase production. This increase in production will soon offset helpers' salaries, or installation costs for labor-saving machinery.
Why should women workers be penalized by lower wage rates because
employers change to more efficient production and management methods, changes which are often long over-due?

Away from the job the woman wage earner must face the consequences of a double wage standard. She must try to buy what she
needs with her smaller earnings. The worn out notion that women
work for "extras" was never more untrue than it is now. According to
Women's Bureau studies made before the war, an unbelievably large
proportion of the women wage earners in this country are the partial
support—many the sole support—of one or more dependents. . . .

There is no "sex differential" when men and women spend the money they earn. Grocery stores do not have double-standard price tags, one for men customers, one for women. A loaf of bread is just a loaf of bread and sells for so much. It makes no difference whether a woman pays for it or a man. The price of meat, potatoes, eggs, coffee, milk—of everything human beings eat—are based on the quality and quantity of the products, not on the sex of the customer.

Landlords charge rent for the house. If a man pays the rent or if a woman pays it, the rent is still the same.

It takes a nickel for a 5 cent telephone call no matter who makes it. There are no special 3 cent slots for a woman's telephone call. . . .

In other words, when women wage earners go to buy food, clothing, and shelter, and to pay taxes, they find no price differential equal to their wage differential.

By setting wage rates for women lower than for men we set in motion the whole vicious cycle of substandard existence: Lower pay means lower standards of living, lower standards of living mean lower productive capacities and lower morale. All of these mean that tax payers must carry a heavier burden. Not only the worker herself but her dependents as well are caught in the consequences of wage differentials for women.

The induction of millions of women into war employment is, in itself, a tremendous undertaking. But the war emergency must not be used to see to it that we maintain basic work standards which experience has shown are necessary for the health and efficiency of all our workers, the standards which result in maximum production. Nor can we merely hold fast, we must go forward. Equality of opportunity must have meaning for women in the shop—their pay rates must be based on their jobs without artificial discrimination based on sex. "Our democratic way of life" must reach into the everyday experience of millions of men and women through organization of workers into strong unions, through collective bargaining and the other democratic methods of self-government in the [union] shop. In all of this, women must carry their full share of the load—do more than pay dues—serve on grievance committees, negotiate wage contracts, work on labor-management committees wherever they are set up. . . .

Bessie Kemp

It is apparent to the women that the tasks before us are great and our future as a nation is at stake. The potentialities of women are being recognized now as never before. It is our problem to utilize these women.

In my shop we have a labor-management committee and two weeks ago a woman was chosen as chairman of that committee. In our shop we have some women who did not know that a woman could head a labor production committee; that is one thing that women have to do in the shop today. It is becoming necessary for us to train women for chief stewards.

Organized labor has taken a definite stand in both peace and war times in democracy and by that I mean a true democracy. According to the President's Executive Order there is to be no discrimination of any kind. Being a negro woman, I am more concerned with the negro women. The CIO[1] has done more throughout the entire country to train and development negro workers than any other union in the country. Our Management would not [hire] any negro girls and our organization asked them why, and they said the workers would object. They have never worked with the people and did not know what it was like to work with them. Today I am a steward in that shop; there are two of us. I was elected to the Industrial CIO Council in New York and so far I haven't participated much in that because I don't feel I am quite able to cope with it just now, but I am learning.

I have been approached many times and asked how a negro feels in a union and I am proud to say that I belong to the UE and I will do everything I can to get the people to do their part. I think it is people like this union that will help in the winning of this war.

---

[1]Congress of Industrial Organizations, an umbrella organization that included the UE.

19

Proceedings of the Seventh Convention of the United Automobile, Aircraft and Agricultural Implement Workers of America

1942

The UAW's conventions during the war years adopted a number of resolutions that addressed issues of concern to women workers. The

---

"Proceedings of the Seventh Convention of the United Automobile, Aircraft and Agricultural Implement Workers of America (UAW-CIO)," (UAW, 1942), 356–61.

following extracts from the 1942 convention gives the text of a successful resolution on wage rate discrimination, as well as delegates Irene Young's and Louella Robinson's comments in favor of it.

Wage Rate Discrimination

. . . WHEREAS: Discrimination because of race, sex, color and creed is inconsistent with the principles of the UAW CIO; and

WHEREAS: Many corporations have pursued a consistent policy of discrimination in establishing rates of pay for women workers; and

WHEREAS: This discrimination is contrary both to the principles of the UAW CIO and the demands of the war effort which will require increasingly employment of women;

THEREFORE BE IT RESOLVED: That this Convention reaffirms the UAW CIO's adherence to the principles of equal pay for equal work; and

BE IT FURTHER RESOLVED: That all local unions be advised to take immediate steps toward the complete elimination of discriminatory differential in rates of pay which now exist. . . .

Delegate Irene Young, Local 174: Mr. Chairman and fellow delegates, this resolution, although it is a good one, will not solve the situation facing thousands of women who are going to be brought into industry in the next few months. I feel that there should be a clause in this resolution that has some teeth in it. I mean by that that at the present time there is nothing here we do not know. We know the CIO position on equal pay for women; we know the government's position on equal pay for women. But so far there are one or two little things we haven't been able to convince management of.

In the plant I came from, in particular, we have thousands of women who in the past have been working on jobs that were practically identical with men's jobs, and yet because there was the word "similar" in there, we have never been able to break this thing down. We have had women working on practically every type of machine that men work on, where the women's top rate was 85 cents and the men ranged all the way from 25 to 50 cents over that.

Women in Industry

In the next few months we are going to have thousands upon thousands of women brought into industry. These women will come from bakeries, beauty shops, restaurants and all other kinds of employment, where the rates are very, very low. If these women are brought into industry at 80 and 90 cent rates they will feel pretty well satisfied with them, and I think this question has to be settled and settled before that influx of women, because once you get these women at 40 or 45 cents higher pay than they have been used to they will think it is a lot. We women who have been in industry ten or fifteen years have battled for an awfully long time, and we have been discriminated against in the matter of wages.

No Square Deal

In those places where the women can see that they are doing exactly the same jobs that the men are, there always has been a feeling among the women that they have not been getting a square deal in this thing, and I think, if we are ever going to get it, now is the time. I think a clause should be inserted in this resolution that no contract can be signed so long as there is a wage differential between men and women.

I feel in connection with this same thing that there are other problems to be solved. In the past where women have been brought in on jobs where the rates were equal to those given the men you had a feeling among the men that women were taking their work away from them. That feeling has been manifested at every convention I have attended; the feeling that women were taking the men's jobs away from them, and the men wanted to have the women kicked out of the shop. I think this is another point where we can convince the men that we are not trying to take their jobs away from them. We have a definite part to play; we are part of this democracy, and we do all we can in order to build the union. We have a place in the union, not only in the bottom of it but in the leadership of the union. We do not want you to discriminate against the men and take their jobs away from them by permitting women to scab for lower pay. Let us get a clause in this thing whereby any contract will not be signed that does not have a clause inserted that there will be no differential in wages between male and female.

Delegate Louella Robinson, Local 785: I agree with everything that this sister delegate has said, and I might add that the first thing I feel we have to do is to convince the men in our union that the women are really worth what the men are. It seems to me that most men feel that women are a little inferior to them and cannot quite produce the work they do.

Well, in our shop, which is in the aircraft industry, it seems to me on our work, women not only equal men but sometimes they surpass them in production. . . .

A lot of men think this question is not important, but it seems to me with the war going on, with the men being taken into the Army, that maybe it will be your wife that will have to be the wage earner in the family. If it were brought home to your family you would want your wife to receive equal pay, because if you are in the Army somebody is going to have to take over.

Men Should Back Women

Another thing, if women are given less pay, when the men do come back from the war they will have to start all over on the low wage rate and build up again. That is one reason why I feel the men should back the women up in this. Maybe this year we are a minority, but perhaps next year we won't be so much that way.

Another argument that is very good, if a woman goes in a restaurant and buys a meal, do they lower the price when they bring the food bill around? No; she pays exactly the same, even if she does make less money to get it.

20

Proceedings of the Eighth International Convention of the United Electrical, Radio and Machine Workers of America

1942

The United Electrical, Radio and Machine Workers of America was particularly attuned to the issues facing women at work. Forty percent of its membership were women, a factor that may have made the industry and the union quicker to promote women's employment in defense industries in the war years. In the following excerpt from the union's 1942 national convention, delegates responded to a resolution calling for training more women to serve as union leaders. The resolution passed.

"Proceedings of the Eighth International Convention of the United Electrical, Radio and Machine Workers of America," 1942, 205–6.

Resolution: Training Women for Union Membership

WHEREAS: (1) the war effort requires mobilization of the broadest sections of our people in active participation in the war effort; and

(2) hundreds of thousands of new women workers are entering our industry, and their organization into trade unions is necessary if they are to produce to the full extent of their ability, and if the interests of both the men and the women workers are to be protected; and

(3) increasing numbers of our men, including large numbers of our leaders, have entered and will continue to enter the armed services of our country; therefore be it

RESOLVED: (1) that special attention be devoted to encouraging women to participate more actively as rank-and-file members and in all positions of leadership; and

(2) that this Convention recommend to all Locals and districts the development of a program of special activities, trade union education, and training for union leadership among women to the end that they may play a more effective part, such as women in the countries of our fighting Allies—Great Britain, the Soviet Union, and China—in the all-out war against Fascism. . . .

Delegate Ruth Wellman (UE Local 1227): In District 4 there was a program for the training in the leadership of local unions, and in my local we also had classes for training women in leadership in the local. There have been concrete results from both those training courses.

We may feel that women have not been experienced in conducting trade union affairs.

They have been rather discouraged and shoved into positions as recording secretaries or perhaps social activities or maybe house committees to clean the windows.

Now, as it is evidenced in this convention, already we have more women who are going to have to take their places on all committees of the union and in all the activities of the union.

The thirteen women on full-time jobs in this International Union is just a beginning. We have a situation where we are going to lose a good many organizers, we are going to lose a good many business agents, our committee members, our stewards, we are losing large sections of all of them. Unless you men get busy and see that they get the help, the encouragement, and the training that they need to take these jobs when your young men go into the army, you are the ones that are going to suffer most.

We are not fighting just for women; we are fighting to preserve all the standards that this Union has built up.

If you don't train people to replace the ones you are going to lose, then it is going to be the men as well as the women who are going to suffer! (Applause). . . .

Delegate Bessie Kemp (UE Local 1225): . . . Our local has been keeping pace and gaining leadership among the locals of District 4 because of its democratic and progressive activities.

As a woman defense-worker, among hundreds like myself in the District, I am doing my share towards aiding the war effort through the tireless efforts of our District to maintain and fit women to take their places in industry.

Months before the attack on Pearl Harbor, the District foresaw the menace that would eventually strike our country.

The result was the calling of a conference in Newark, New Jersey. This conference was held to facilitate the training of women in industry, if and when war was declared. Out of the conference a gigantic program was started; first an education program for women was to be set up to prepare women for leadership in the Union. Training classes were started for women in order to develop trained, skilled workers in the defense plants and a campaign for equal pay for equal work done and a determination to take a definite stand against discrimination.

After the attack on Pearl Harbor a meeting was held in UE locals and in Local 1225, with Ruth Young and other trade union advisers to discuss the urgent need for training women and the types of skills to be taught. As a result of this important meeting, classes were started immediately for girls, among whom were one-third Negroes.

Since that time, District 4 can be justly proud of its women who have taken their places on the assembly line and proven themselves conscientious and reliable workers. They are purchasing bonds and stamps, contributing towards Allied War Relief, keeping in touch with the boys in the armed forces, donating their blood and doing everything possible and their fullest in the winning of the war. . . .

Delegate Lottie Lieb (Local 601): . . . A death-struggle is being waged by vast armies to determine whether slavery shall rule or, when peace has been declared, whether we shall be able to build on the foundations of human freedom, liberty and equality — certainly a major development of this war and a shining light to our allied people as we march to victory.

If our men are valiantly fighting for these principles, so have we women realized long ago that the happiness of every family in this country depends upon the complete victory over dictatorship, over the Nazi scourge of all humanity, with its principles of race hatred, exploiting of foreign lands, and its subjugation of women.

Today woman's place has been definitely established.

If, in the past, the place assigned to her was more or less limited and only specific types of work designated to so-called woman's work, women have shown that they are capable of fighting shoulder to shoulder for the principles they believe in. Women have shown especially so in industry, through the medium of organized labor. Woman's place has altered virtually over night from the secondary lines of defense in so-called inferior jobs to the front lines of equality.

Here we must admit if the term equality had been really applied to women today it would be an advantage to us if women today would not have to act as apprentices and amateurs.

However, let us progressively march forward, taking our rightful place in the economic and political life of our country, and as we are doing everything towards the defeat of Fascism, so must we stamp out completely any medieval ideas that are identified with Fascism, and one of these, fellow workers, is the subjugation of women.

21

AUGUSTA CHRONICLE

Rosie the Riveter Wants Man's Pay, Lady's Respect
December 11, 1944

Union women demands for equal pay received extensive media coverage. This 1944 Associated Press newspaper article addresses the question of the seeming contradiction between the women leaders' support for protective legislation, opposition to the Equal Rights Amendment, and the demand for equal pay.

"Rosie the Riveter Wants Man's Pay, Lady's Respect," *Augusta Chronicle*, December 11, 1944, A-8.

Rosie the riveter wants a man's pay, but she expects industry to treat her like a lady for all that.

The 150 delegates to the first national women's conference of the United Automobile Workers (CIO) made that quite plain yesterday.

All that was needed to undam a torrent of feminine opinion on the subject was the suggestion of a speaker (male) that if Rosie wants equal pay for equal work she also should expect to turn out the same quality and quantity of work and observe the same conduct as a man.

The speaker, the UAW's own Thomas A. Johnstone, acting director of the union's General Motors department, had the further temerity to suggest that rivetin' Rosie, for the sake of a man's pay, might have to give up some of the little privileges accorded her by employer and fellow-employe alike in deference to her sex.

"If women insist on getting the same rate of pay plus rest periods, which men do not get, then the men will raise a little hell," Johnstone bravely said.

That was all the ladies needed. One delegate after another leaped to her feet and forcefully recounted her experiences and beliefs. Here are some of the things they said.

"A man worker would not expect his wife or sister to do heavy lifting."

"My job is one that a man would throw across the room if he worked on it an hour."

"Brawn should not be considered more important than brains."

"I know plenty of men workers who have more time off the floor than the women do."

"Management says women need close supervision. Do they? Well, as for my superior you can take him and send him to Saipan. Supervisors stir up more trouble than help—and some of them certainly give certain women workers preferential treatment."

The delegates adopted a resolution designed to spur the UAW-CIO executive board in the fight for equal pay for equal work; another urging abolition of separate job classifications for women; one pressing grievances in plants where merit advancement to the top brackets is denied women workers; another advocating regularly scheduled, paid rest periods—two 15-minute siestas—for all workers and still another asking 45 minutes for lunch with adequate "wash-up time."

The conference also went on record in opposition to the proposed equal rights amendment to the federal constitution, on the ground that it would void state legislation governing working conditions for women.

22

AMMUNITION

Cover: Women Work / Women Vote

August 1944

A remarkable indication of the sense that women could be mobilized as voters to support working class causes in electoral politics emerged clearly in a special issue of the UAW-CIO's journal, Ammunition, *published in August 1944. The articles addressed women's activity in unions and drew attention to issues of importance to them as voters, as the magazine's cover image suggests.*

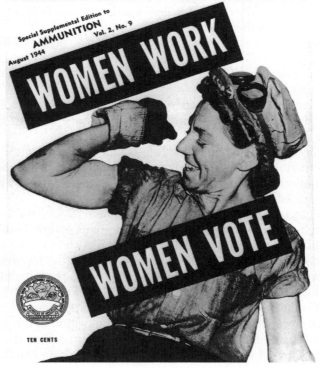

Courtesy United Auto Workers (UAW)

AMMUNITION

And We Say—

August 1944

The August 1944 special issue of the UAW's journal, Ammunition, *urged women to be politically active on a range of issues. The article below follows a piece written by First Lady Eleanor Roosevelt, entitled "Eleanor Roosevelt* Says*—."*

EVERY WOMAN IN YOUR LOCAL, IN YOUR PLANT, IS INTERESTED IN SOME OR ALL OF THE SHOP PROBLEMS TOUCHED UPON IN THE FOLLOWING PAGES. EVERY WOMAN IN YOUR LOCAL IS INTERESTED IN THE PRICE OF FOOD, CLOTHES, AND HOUSING, IN CONSUMER PROGRAMS.

There is no woman in our local who doesn't want to vote right in the next election, no woman who does not want to become a good union member. But plenty of women do not know they want this.

Many women do not know what the union has already done for them, what it can do for them if they become active. Many do not know that a large proportion of their shop grievances are ultimately settled in the state legislature or in Washington. Some do not fully realize that the grievances they have outside the shop—prices, the soldier vote, a possible lack of jobs after the war—that all the grief will increase a thousandfold unless they vote right; that only by electing the right President, congressmen, state legislators, and other "public servants" will the interests of the majority of the people be served.

Unless every active union member works overtime on political action today, neither they nor anyone else in the country will have any assurance of a job or a union tomorrow. We have been lax in educating, even at times in organizing, the women in our shops. Now we are faced with the necessity of making absolutely certain every woman in every shop votes for the best interest of herself and the majority of the people. It's a rush job, but it can be done and must get done if we are to have any security for the next years.

There are thousands of active, competent women union members and leaders. What has been accomplished by, and with, women in some locals can be accomplished in all locals. The strength of the union now and of

"And We Say—," *Ammunition* 2, no. 9 (August 1944): 1.

the whole labor movement later depends to a great extent on the job we do today in activizing [*sic*] all women politically. For to the extent that job is well done, we shall have laid a solid groundwork for making all working women into good, understanding, active union members and citizens. If we fail in completing this work, we shall have weakened the labor movement and by doing so weakened the greatest democratic force in America.

24

AMMUNITION

You Have Only One Life to Live
August 1944

The following article from the same issue specifically encourages women's activism in support of the enforcement of health and safety laws.

NINETY-NINE CHANCES OUT OF A HUNDRED SOME HEALTH OR SAFETY LAW IS BEING BROKEN IN YOUR SHOP.

But if you don't know what the law is, what can you do about it? You can:
WRITE: To your State Department of Labor for all laws and regulations covering health and safety hazards, hours, rest periods, lunch periods, and sanitary conditions.
WRITE: To the Women's Bureau of the U.S. Department of Labor, Washington, D.C., for their recommendations and standards on these problems. . . .
NOW, SISTERS, LET'S STOP GRIPING AND ACT. With the existent legal possibilities for obtaining healthy and safe working conditions, by working together, we should get them. Consult your union grievance committee. Submit plenty of policy grievances. Get advice from the UAW Research Department if need be.

ELECT A CONGRESS AND STATE LEGISLATURES WHICH WILL PASS THE KIND OF LAWS WHICH ASSURE YOU AND ALL WORKERS LONG, HEALTHY LIVES.

The proposed Equal Rights Amendment to the Constitution of the United States would destroy state wage and hour laws, and health legislation for women. (For further information and action to be taken against this amendment, write the Congress of Women's Auxiliaries of the CIO). . . . THIS AMENDMENT MUST BE KILLED!

"You Have Only One Life to Live," *Ammunition* 2, no. 9 (August 1944): 18.

AMMUNITION

What Do You Care about Children?

August 1944

In keeping with union women's interest in addressing problems that specifically affect women workers, the following article addresses state-funded childcare.

Care has been provided for the children of war-working mothers through private schools; with the assistance of welfare agencies financed by private donations; through city, state, and federal funds, singly and in combination.

Still it is generally agreed that only about one-third of the total number of children needing care have received it. The fact that the children of our nation have been neglected in wartime is clearly the fault of the voting population of the nation.

Those of us who in the past allowed the election to public office of men, or women, who voted against the use of public money for the care of our children—all of us who permitted these people to have a voice in government—are guilty of having hurt our own children and every child in the nation.

The Federal Funds for child care appropriated under the Lanham Act and distributed by the Federal Works Agency have been inadequate. But within the limit of those funds here and there in the USA, funds for the following kinds of services have been made available:

1. Group care for infants under two years of age.
2. Group care for children from two up through all the ages covered by the public schools.
3. Maintenance and expansion of normal school services in congested areas.
4. Recreational programs where existing facilities are inadequate.

"What Do You Care about Children?" *Ammunition* 2, no. 9 (August 1944): 26.

5. Assistance to public health authorities in the treatment of venereally infected persons. (The average of girls treated in such centers is 18, many being much younger).

6. Protective services, such as policemen and policewomen.

There is not a single CIO local which is situated where there is not need for more and better child care facilities.

IF WE IN NOVEMBER RE-ELECT ANY OF THOSE PEOPLE TO PUBLIC OFFICE WHO HAVE NOT FAVORED THE APPROPRIATION OF ALL THE PUBLIC MONEY NECESSARY FOR THE CARE OF THE NATION'S CHILDREN IN WARTIME, AND HAVE NOT BACKED FULLY ANY VITAL PROPOSED PROGRAM AT ANY LEVEL, IF WE ELECT ANYONE TO PUBLIC OFFICE WHO WILL NOT AT ANY TIME, IN PEACE OR WAR, FAVOR SUCH EXPENDITURES AND PROGRAMS, WE SHALL HAVE COMMITTED A CARDINAL SIN AGAINST OUR OWN CHILDREN AND EVERY CHILD IN THE NATION.

Check the records of everyone for whom you are going to vote in November. Patting babies on the head is not evidence that your public servant will heed your wishes when it comes to voting for appropriations or installing good school programs.

26

Report of the UAW-CIO's Women's Conference
December 1944

Both the UE and the UAW organized conferences during the war to promote women's leadership and to address women workers' issues (see Documents 19 and 20). In December 1944, the UAW's Women's Department held a conference in Detroit that included commentary about postwar work issues and women workers. The following extract is from the conference report and hints at the ways in which union women would seek to protect women's rights as workers when the war ended. Despite their attempts, women were often frustrated in their postwar efforts.

"Report of UAW-CIO Women's Conference to International Executive Board," United Auto Worker War Policy Division, Victor Reuther Collection, Box 2, Folder: "Conferences," Wayne State University (Detroit, December 8–9, 1944).

STAFF MEMBERS

WHEREAS: Women workers have made a major contribution not only to our war production, but also strengthened the entire labor movement and our Democracy through their activities in the political action program; and

WHEREAS:

1. There are 300,000 women members in the UAW-CIO at the present time, and surveys made by the UAW and other unions, government agencies and management show that a large percentage of women wish to remain in the plants after the war. As Mrs. Eleanor Roosevelt stated in her message to the Conference, "Many women will find themselves obliged to work, some because they have become permanent breadwinners, and others because they are not confronted with the necessity of giving more time to their homes and find work both interesting and worthwhile."

2. The UAW-CIO has indicated that they are in accord with this thinking as is evidenced by our post-war program in which the union advocates jobs for all.

3. One of the purposes of this conference is to set up and effect a program to activize [sic] women and increase their participation in general union activities.

THEREFORE BE IT RESOLVED: That this Conference recommend to the International Executive Board that it urge local unions to set up women's committees to work in cooperation with the Women's Bureau, War Policy Division [of the UAW], to handle special women's problems which are not now being taken care of.

BE IT FURTHER RESOLVED: That the International Executive Board be urged to adopt a policy of making staff appointments on the basis of qualifications and competence and that women be considered on a fair and equal basis without prejudice with men. And further, that when additional women are added to the staff, that they be given assignments comparable to those of other staff members.

BE IT FINALLY RESOLVED: That the International Executive Board encourage local unions and the national corporation department and councils to adopt the same policy.

CONTINUING PROGRAM

WHEREAS:

1. In the transition period following the collapse of Germany, women workers as the newest industrial group, will feel first the impact of contract cancellations and cutbacks. Although our problems will be the same as any other group of workers, women will have unusual and unique difficulties with which to cope. Especially will Negro women, who in many plants have the least seniority, have major readjustments to make. Layoffs, downgrading, unemployment compensation, training opportunities, job placements, women's protective legislation, child welfare are but some of the women's problems which will require special consideration and attention by the International Union.

2. The National UAW-CIO Women's Committee . . . has made a valuable and significant contribution in arranging and planning this Conference.

3. The continuation of this Committee is necessary and desirable for assisting in developing a strong and effective program for meeting UAW-CIO women's problems.

THEREFORE BE
IT RESOLVED:

That this Conference endorses the work of the Women's Bureau,[1] War Policy Division and the National UAW-CIO Women's Committee and recommends to the International Executive Board

1. That the National UAW-CIO Women's Committee be continued.

2. That it authorize the Women's Bureau, War Policy Division . . . to develop a program designed:

   (a) To increase participation of women members in general Union activities.

   (b) To improve work standards in the plants and provide materials on women's activities for the use of active Union women, Local Union officers, bargaining committees and international representatives.

   (c) Provide programs for meeting women's out-plant problems.

---

[1] The Women's Bureau here refers to the UAW's Women's Bureau, not the federal agency.

    (d) To strengthen state and federal legislation pro-
        tecting the rights, working conditions, health
        and safety of women.
    (e) To stimulate women's interest in furthering the
        UAW-CIO program of full employment.[2]
    (f) To promote projects and programs to cushion
        the shock of cutbacks and contract cancella-
        tions, upon women workers.

[2]At the end of the war, the CIO lobbied Congress unsuccessfully for a "full employment bill," which would charge the federal government with creating jobs in times of
significant unemployment.

27

LILLIAN HATCHER

Oral History Account of a UAW Activist
1978–1979

*For a number of union women, their World War II experiences sparked
a lifetime of activism. Lillian Hatcher, a riveter who served as the
assistant director of the UAW's Women's Bureau and on that union's
Fair Practices and Anti-Discrimination committee, worked for the
UAW for almost thirty years and was the UAW's representative to civil
rights organizations. Like many African American workers in this era,
especially those associated with the CIO, Hatcher was impressed with the
way in which union leadership took a stand in defense of black workers.
In this extract from an interview, Hatcher discusses the UAW's response
to white women workers' racism in defense work. (Note: The ellipsis in
this selection is in the original.)*

Hatcher: It was in Packard that there was a hate strike [in 1943]. A very,
    very momentous hate strike at Packard where the white women did
    not want to work with black women. There was a large clientele of
    Polish women at Packard and, of course, Polish people in the city
    of Detroit were in an employment sphere in industry just a tiny step

Lillian Hatcher, interviewed by Lyn Goldfarb and Lorraine Gray, "The Twentieth-
Century Trade Union Woman: Vehicle for Social Change," Oral History Project, Institute
of Labor and Industrial Relations, University of Michigan, 1980, 51–53.

ahead of black workers. They were the foundry workers, they were the people on the broom, they were the last hired, they were the considered low education ratings and so on. And then when the black workers came in, they moved up a little higher into higher brackets of employment or employment codes, whatever codes that would entitle them to higher wages or department structure.

There were many problems involved in the Packard Motor Car Company problems: one of upgrading, one of promotion of black women, then one of some white women not wanting to work with black women, not wanting to break them in on the job, not wanting to share the restrooms, a composite of a number of what I call very un-American activities were prevailing during wartime. Whether or not it was to destroy the morale—that's what I would like to believe—it was more than hate, but they labelled it as hate strikes. I thought it was merely to undermine, not merely, but I thought it was a gimmick, even then, to undermine whatever patriotism we practiced at that time. I thought it was a force in this country that really didn't want to see the workers get along together.

I was not at Packard, so I can't give you the details on that. We had some disturbance, I'll call it, at Ford. And Walter Reuther took a very excellent position on the situation at Ford and also in GM and some of the other places to the point that if a person didn't want to work with black women . . . you had a choice. You could either take your job assignment or you could ring up, ring the clock out.[1] And consequently they rung in and stayed in, most of them did, became good friends. Those who made it to Tennessee every weekend,[2] they were off of vacation (laugh) time, they began to work right along with the other workers, found their place in the union as well. Now this was, took longer time to achieve in some places than it did others. But it did come to pass that Southern workers, black workers, white workers, foreign born or fourth and fifth generation people, did learn to work together. And when we had the first riot in Detroit, 1943,[3] we did not have any strife, so to speak, in the plants. The strife was in the street, but industry worked every day.

[1]Meaning that they could quit.

[2]Hatcher is probably referring to the assumption that these white workers were from the rural south.

[3]Nine whites and twenty-five African Americans were killed in the June 1943 Detroit race riot that erupted over tensions between blacks and whites over housing and employment opportunities.

4

The Second Shift

Among the many challenges facing working women during World War II were the problems associated with the "second shift"—the work that women performed at home after they returned from their paid jobs. In most families, women assumed responsibilities for household chores whether they worked or not. Crowded public transportation, cramped or inadequate housing, rationing, and long work hours added to their problems. And, for women with children, finding adequate childcare was a pressing concern. The pressure from these responsibilities was undoubtedly one of the reasons for absenteeism among women workers. The documents in this chapter address a range of second-shift issues. Note that Documents 28 and 30 are written by well-educated women who understood their work to be temporary. Does that affect their value as sources? To what extent do the documents, especially those dealing with childcare, suggest the persistence of traditional notions of women's role in the home?

28

NELL GILES

Gas Ration Vital to Factory Worker
1942

In June 1942 Nell Giles was a reporter for the Boston Globe *when she took a short-term job making precision instruments at General Electric facilities in West Lynn, Massachusetts, and began her column "Smooth Susan Takes a War Job." She explained she wanted to find out what real*

Nell Giles, "Gas Ration Vital to Factory Worker," *Boston Globe*, July 29, 1942, 15.

workers were doing in contrast to the "pictures of beautiful girls posed on the wings of planes with a glowing caption to make you think that war is glamorous." In the following excerpt, Giles describes a key problem facing women during the second shift, the problem of getting to and from work.

The distance you live from work is the most vital statistic in your life as a factory worker. It determines the number of hours you sleep, the time you have to play, how often you can go to town to spend your money!

If it were possible, all the girls would live in this factory town. Most of them do. For some, it's a 15-minute walk to work. But for hundreds of others, getting to work is a matter of driving for miles.

One girl lives in Haverhill. She gets up between 4 and 4:30 in the morning, is lucky if she has time to eat enough breakfast, rushes to dress and meet her "ride" in time to get her to work three minutes early. Barbara has spent her noon hour for the last month looking for a room to rent near the factory. But the rooming houses and the private homes are filled to capacity. Not a chance has Barbara of finding that "nice little room near work" which would give her time for sufficient sleep and recreation.

One girl lives in a trailer camp . . . [ellipses in original] and I'm surprised there are not more houses on wheels for this concentrated form of life. As a girl in the rest room said the other day, "All we do is sleep and work!" with some disgust, and you can see her point, but isn't it what everyone is doing these days? Never have we seen the importance of physical fitness and especially of sufficient SLEEP more than now.

You try nothing more strenuous than eight hours of sleep and eight hours of work, leaving a slight margin of eight hours for life and transportation. And you'd be amazed at how fast those marginal hours vanish on the cuff! There's always something you hadn't counted on, and then in my case, transportation alone takes three hours a day, and I'm not an exception. You can see that it is sensible to give in quietly and not try to see all your friends or be a social butterfly on the side.

Heinz Ketchup Ad Promising Help with Rationing
1942

All Americans struggled with the dietary limitations created by the government's rationing of foods like butter, meat, wheat, canned goods, eggs, cheese, and sugar. The Office of War Information urged magazines and newspapers to offer suggestions to women defense workers about organizing their time to allow them to take care of household responsibilities generally and about menus and cooking advice. In this 1942 advertisement for Heinz Ketchup, the company cleverly linked its product to women war workers' needs. The vivid red, white, and blue colors in the ad underlined the message of the woman's patriotism.

Sally Edelstein Archive

JANE LYNOTT CARROLL

Raising a Baby on Shifts

October 1943

Childcare was the most pressing issue for working mothers during the war. The solution that Jane Lynott Carroll describes in this article printed in Parents Magazine *was not typical, but it does provide insight into the difficulties families faced in providing care for children when mothers worked. It also conveys the feelings many women felt toward combining motherhood and paid employment.*

Almost every newspaper and magazine we read these days has stories on the controversial subject of mothers working. Among incentives that put mothers in war plants are listed the economic and the patriotic. Both were working in my case. When our baby was two and a half months old, my husband was inducted into the Army. The house payments and the stack of bills on the desk gradually mounted, in spite of my efforts to make the ends of the G.I. check meet.

One day I met a former employer. . . . I remembered that welcome pay check which I spent for luxuries then, but which I needed for necessities now. I thought about it all the way home and finally I called several day nurseries, but found the local ones take only children two years and up. I read advertisements in the papers for private homes where children are kept by the day, but these aren't licensed, as most nurseries are, and I felt uncertain about them.

I considered a private nurse, but in several weeks of negotiation with a half dozen sources, I interviewed only two women whom I felt I would want to intrust my baby for the better part of his waking hours. Nor was there a chance of calling on Grandmother, for both of Billy's grandmothers live 2000 miles away.

The vital point to me, however, in any of these arrangements, was the fact that someone else would feed Billy and sun him, would enjoy his smiles, see his lip-quivering tears. Someone else would teach him his first words and influence that vital forming of habits — while I came home in time to put him to bed.

Jane Lynott Carroll, "Raising a Baby on Shifts," *Parents Magazine* (October 1943), 20, 77, 80.

Then a call to the employment office of the aircraft plant nearest our home assured me that women were hired for the graveyard shift, from 12:30 A.M. to 7:00 A.M. — a period two hours shorter than the regular eight-hour-plus-lunchtime day shifts, but received equal pay. This suited my purpose exactly, for the baby would be asleep during those hours anyway. When I had worked out my plan, I wrote to my best friend and college roommate, explained it to her and asked her to join forces with me.

Sue, who had been following her soldier husband around from post to post, boarding house to furnished apartment until he was sent overseas, had no household impedimenta to dispose of and thought the idea perfect. A week later she arrived to live with me and we applied for jobs at the same plant, she as a stenographer on the 8:00 to 4:30 office shift, and I on the graveyard shift.

We started work the next day and our home slipped into the shifts as well-defined as those of the plant. I found I liked my factory work much better than some of the secretarial jobs I had held. I work steadily, and when the whistle blows, I am free to forget my job and devote myself to my home and to the raising and enjoying of my baby. . . .

[Carroll offers details of the schedule that gives her ample time to care for her child. She also describes the division of household tasks like cleaning and laundry.]

Of course, the silver is not polished weekly, as it used to be; my once-busy knitting needles are lying quietly in an empty knitting bag, and hot rolls and other time-consuming pastry concoctions are picked up at the local bakery. But on the whole, I believe our home is as well run as are many homes of full-time mothers who don't budget their time and who just "never seem to get around to" reading books, playing with their children, and enjoying the homes and yards in which they "slave" unseeing from morning to night. Many mothers feel tied down in their homes with their babies, while their husbands are out in the world all day. But a working mother is glad to get home and really enjoy its comforts and, yes, even its problems. . . .

I am not criticizing regular mothers, for I think they do full-time jobs, and I know I couldn't run both my jobs alone. But as Sue and I figure it, we are two persons with three jobs. Our extra half-job apiece takes the place of the time we used to spend with our husbands and keeps us so busy we can't worry and brood.

And when Billy is old enough, I believe he will be enjoying every baby's birthright, a mother *and* father, and perhaps a little sister or brother too. Our mode of life is for the duration. It isn't an easy life, but the inconveniences are made up for by the knowledge that my baby isn't missing any of this mother's care and love to which he is entitled. I'm proud to be able to provide for him and at the same time help his Daddy, as well as a lot of other Daddies.

31

MARYE STUMPH

Oral History Account of an Aviation Worker's Solution to Childcare
1982

Marye Stumph was a divorcée with two children when she decided to leave her home in Ohio to look for better economic opportunities in the West. In 1941, she got a war job at Vultee Aircraft Company in Long Beach, California, and for a few months placed her children in an institution called the Children's Home Society in Hollywood. In this extract from her oral history, she describes how she solved the childcare responsibilities for herself and a fellow worker.

As soon as I got enough for a month's rent, I rented a little house in Long Beach. . . . With the children's ages, I needed somebody around when I was at work. My mother had been living up in the country, and she came down to visit me and decided to stay. So the four of us lived together. I paid twenty dollars a month and it was four rooms. One room was pretty small, but we made it Bill's bedroom and Mama had a bedroom and Carol and I slept on the davenport in the living room. It was very comfortable and it had a little kitchen. It worked out real well for us. I felt safe about working and leaving the kids with her and she managed things at home. I wasn't able to save anything, not right then. It was just sort of live from payday to payday.

We kind of felt the need of making a little more money than we'd get just from wages, so we got a larger place and boarded a couple of young children. We went through the city of Long Beach and got a foster home license. This woman was working in a defense plant and

Sherna Berger Gluck, *Rosie the Riveter Revisited: Women, the War, and Social Change* (New York: New American Library, 1987), 64.

she needed somebody to take care of her children. One child was just a baby, less than a year old; another little boy was about three. They stayed and slept there and she'd come to visit them. Mama managed real well and it made us a little extra money.

32

RAYMOND CLAPPER

Home Chores Bothering War Workers

September 30, 1943

This 1943 syndicated newspaper article summed up many of the problems facing working women and offered suggestions for improving the absentee problem. Raymond Clapper cites the recommendations of Alan Johnstone, representative of the Federal Works Agency, which was the federal agency that provided childcare for defense workers under the Lanham Act.

Every family knows how much time is consumed now in shopping, in attending to paper work in connection with rationing and in other bare essentials of daily living.

For a housewife to get through the daily routine now requires nothing so much as time and good feet for walking and waiting.

Absenteeism among women being about nine times that of men, I wonder if there is some connection between absence from work and the difficulty of attending to a housewife's routine duties.

Those who are working on the problem of Pacific Coast manpower troubles in aircraft factories are beginning to look hard at some household problems. In one Lockheed-Vega plant, 25 percent of the 40,000 women employed are mothers. Absenteeism among mother is the most serious problem, not because they are tired, or lazy, but most often because they must have time out to take care of the children, to take them to the doctor, or to buy shoes, or for any one of scores of reasons that any mother could give you.

A lot of our manpower trouble is just as simple as that.

Raymond Clapper, "Home Chores Bothering War Workers," *Dallas Morning News*, September 30, 1943, 3.

Child Care Centers

Alan Johnstone, general counsel of the Federal Works Agency, has been in consultation with aircraft production men, such as Henry J. Kaiser, and with others concerned. Particularly between himself and Kaiser, some suggestions are being developed that may ease the burden of wives and mothers so that they can give more complete time to their jobs. But it will require the government to assist in doing what will be sneeringly described by some as social work, so perhaps the idea will be damned from the start for that reason. A number of things are suggested as a result of the investigations of Johnstone to reduce greatly the amount of lost time, especially among women.

Child care centers, not free, but underwritten in part, are needed wherever large numbers of mothers are working. Medical and dental facilities are needed near war plants for employees and their families to eliminate time-consuming trips downtown.

Shopping facilities especially are needed near plants. That would avoid much absence incurred by employees to purchase groceries, meat, general household supplies and work clothes. Barbershops and beauty parlors are needed. Merchants cannot remain open after working hours, of if they can, stocks of necessities are likely to be depleted at late hours. An OPA [Office of Price Administration] or rationing board agent should be present to facilitate all ration book and coupon transactions. An hour lost in attending to ration routine is an hour lost from producing bombers. Established business firms, at the various localities, would readily co-operate if facilities were available for lease, Johnstone says.

Banking Facilities

Banking facilities are badly needed near war plants, not only to deposit and cash checks, but as a means of paying rent, electric light, gas, milk and all other regular family accounts for services. Branches of laundry, dry cleaning, shoe repairing, drugstore and similar requirements could be installed to operate principally on a leave-and-call basis. Employees['] rental and real-estate services are needed.

Employers say that women workers are held in the highest esteem. But women must purchase, cook and provide food for their families, do the household washing, pay sundry bills, care for their children, attend the family medical and dental needs, and whatever time can be saved them will reduce their absences for vital war production.

The Federal Works Agency is authorized to provide facilities necessary for carrying on the community life where it is expanded by war,

and some of its officials, notable Johnstone, have under consideration a
project to help start services of the kind outlined above.

33

JANE EADS

Drafting of Fathers Spurs Federal Child Care Program

October 17, 1943

The following month, another syndicated article focused on the childcare problem. Associated Press staff writer Jane Eads reports on the proposed Thomas Bill, which childcare professionals hoped to pass in order to give the Children's Bureau and the federal Office of Education oversight over federal childcare programs. The programs would be federally subsidized but directed by the states. The Bureau was particularly eager to implement foster home care as an alternative to nurseries for small children. The bill ultimately failed and the Federal Works Agency continued to direct childcare programs. The article, however, offers valuable insight into attitudes toward working mothers as well as toward institutionalized childcare.

Their mothers work . . . [Ellipses in original]

The children found crying with the cold, or hungry, locked in cars all day on parking lots, tied to the furniture in empty apartments, aimlessly roaming the streets— armies of "floating" children. . . .

These children have had no adult to look after them. The children's bureau, the department of labor, the office of education and other groups concerned with the welfare of children are looking for an immediate remedy.

They warn that an already serious problem will be multiplied this year with the drafting of 446,000 fathers and the need for mothers to take jobs to supplement the allowances they'll be getting from the government.

Unless care is provided for the children of working mothers, these agencies declare, the full energies of the nation's womanpower can't be utilized, and absenteeism, juvenile delinquency and "floating" children will hinder the war effort.

Jane Eads, "Drafting of Fathers Spurs Federal Child Care Program," *Tampa Bay Times*, October 17, 1943, 13.

To "increase efficiency of employed mothers, reduce absenteeism, to curb neglect of children and allay the anxiety of mothers," the agencies ask [for] a comprehensive child care program providing for health, recreation, education and general welfare in a variety of services to meet the varying needs of families.

The agencies declare the "war area child care act of 1943," supported by the president and already passed by the senate would fill the bill.

This measure, introduced in congress by Senator Elbert Thomas of Utah, would provide a federal appropriation of $20,000,000 a year for operation of state-directed child care programs.

The office of education and the states already have formulated unified state programs and are ready to put local plans into action.

The bill would provide for supervision of foster homes where mothers take care of other women's children, a counseling service to working mothers, and before-and-after-school care of school-age children.

The program would cover children under 16, living in war industry areas, whose mothers are employed in any of the various activities essential to the war.

The agencies say passage of the Thomas bill would not mean federal control of child-care programs. The funds would be administered by the children's bureau and the office of education, but existing public and private agencies would be utilized. . . . The state agencies in co-operation with the local authorities would be given full responsibility for planning and carrying out their programs.

Supporters of the bill point out that up until now there has been no legislation defining the scope of federal participation in state or local programs to provide for children of employed mothers. Communities, however, have received some federal aid through the Lanham act for community facilities administered by the federal works agency (FWA).

Maj. Gen. Philip B. Fleming, director of FWA, recently reported that its child care centers were operating at less than one-fourth of their capacity.

Why?

A committee representing nine of the country's leading women's organizations, the children's bureau and the office of education reports these reasons:

1. Nursery schools have been improperly located, sometimes where there was not enough demand for womanpower and sometimes too far from plants where women work so that transportation has presented serious difficulties.
2. Limited hours of service in many of these centers fail to provide for the needs of mothers who work long hours.

3. Mothers have not been informed of the existence of convenient nurseries.
4. Many mothers feel that the nurseries are tied up with "relief."

Supporters of the Thomas bill also point out that the Lanham act makes no provisions for funds for programs such as foster family home services which a large number of working mothers seem to prefer, for advisory services for mothers or health services for their children.

Although the war manpower commission has discouraged employment of women responsible for the care of young children, the women's committee reports that large numbers of mothers "through economic necessity, anxiety, or eagerness to use their skills in behalf of the war, have taken employment and are continuing to do so."

The children's bureau estimates that about one-third of working mothers need care for their children, and adds that no one kind of care can solve this problem, that a variety of facilities is needed for children of different ages.

34

SURVEY MIDMONTHLY

Kaiser's Children

December 1944

The most innovative approach to childcare for defense workers came from Henry J. Kaiser, who established childcare centers at his shipyards in Portland, Oregon, and Richmond, California. Estimates are that the centers served about 1,000 children over the course of the war. When interviewed by the New York Times *in 1943 shortly before two of his centers opened, Kaiser argued that women were in the factory workforce to stay and it was time to address their needs, including childcare. However, with war's end and the end of federal subsidies, Kaiser closed the centers. The program received favorable publicity and an award from* Parents Magazine. *Yet, even professionals who wrote approvingly of the Kaiser experiment questioned its permanence, as this article from* Survey Midmonthly *makes clear.*

"Kaiser's Children," *Survey Midmonthly* 80 (December 1944): 351.

When Henry Kaiser opened child care centers in his Portland, Ore., shipyards a year ago, many a social work eyebrow was raised at this example of industrial paternalism. Child care centers, said the purists, should be community sponsored projects, and they hinted that shipbuilders should stick to their shipbuilding.

In a sense, that is just what Mr. Kaiser was doing, for he knew that efficient work among the women employed in his yards depended largely on their peace of mind. If their minds were relieved of worry about what might be happening to their children, they would be free to concentrate on their jobs. And if care were available at their place of work, they would be spared the enervating experience of having to take their children someplace else and call for them every day before and after work. The U.S. Maritime Commission agreed with Mr. Kaiser and built the two large, modernly equipped nurseries for him at the Swan Island and Oregon Shipyards.

Last month as the centers passed their first anniversary, attendance statistics told the story of their success. Like other child care centers throughout the country during the first few months of operations, they found little demand for their services. In fact, for nearly six months attendance remained low, for a while averaging only 183 children a week. Last month, however, the centers were caring for 680 children a week. This upswing in attendance, according to James L. Hymes, Jr., manager of the shipyard's child service department, indicates two things about working mothers: that they must be educated in the use of group care for their children and that they will not enroll their children in any institution until they have seen it in operation.

Mr. Hymes has pointed out that since management also learns by experience, changes have been made in the centers' operations from time to time as needs have become obvious. For example, they are now open on a twenty-four hour basis in order to serve mothers of any of the three shifts. They have also instituted a hot dish service so that a mother can pick up the main course of the family's evening meal when calling for her child.

Whether or not this type of child care service holds any promise for the future is open to question. Because these are wartimes it can be welcomed because of the rapidity and efficiency with which it can be got under way to meet two immediate needs: reducing absenteeism in the plants and releasing more women for war work. But after the war the whole subject of the care of children of working mothers will have to be reconsidered. More weight can be given then to the argument that the young child's place is in his home with his mother.

5

Women in Uniform

Patriotism was undoubtedly a key factor in inducing American women to volunteer for the armed services during World War II. So, too, was the desire for travel and adventure. Nisei women in Hawaii, for example, described yearning to see the continental United States as part of the reason for their enlistment. Other women hoped to serve abroad. Although military work was far more regimented than civilian jobs, it was also a form of employment. Whatever women's personal goals, the media often focused on their femininity, thus reinforcing the widespread ambivalence about women in the military. Drawing upon the documents presented here, what conclusions can you draw about why women joined the military? How did the media portray these enlistees? What challenges did African American military women face?

35

SATURDAY EVENING POST

Women of Two Wars
May 29, 1943

The media paid much attention to women's military uniforms during World Wars I and II, not surprisingly since military uniforms were traditionally a powerful symbol of male citizenship. This 1943 article featured two full colored pages of uniforms for both World War I and World War II. The emphasis on femininity for World War II–era uniforms was in

"Women of Two Wars," *Saturday Evening Post* 215 (May 29, 1943): 26.

keeping with the recruitment advertisements that often featured glamorous looking women in attractive uniforms, a tactic that minimized the threat uniformed women might pose to conventional notions of women's proper roles. Although magazines and newspapers did feature more serious stories about the types of work and contributions military women made to the war effort, the somewhat flippant tone in this article was also typical.

[Since World War I] the number and variety [of women in uniform] are greater. Women's standing in the armed services has gone up—and so have their wardrobes.

Take the Navy Nurse Corps. It was just plain "Nurse" in the last war; they had no military titles. The only official regalia were white ward uniforms and navy blue capes for hospital duty. Elsewhere they wore their own civilian clothes, although street uniforms were finally issued for identification overseas and, by the armistice, worn by chief nurses in the country as well as abroad. Well, today they have officer's rank, starting out as ensigns. In addition to hospital costumes, there are winter and summer street uniforms for all, sweaters and sundry accessories.

Army nurses have gone through a similar metamorphosis from civilian to commissioned-officer status, beginning at second lieutenant, from mere hospital outfits to dress uniforms and all the fixings. . . .

The new street uniforms of the Army nurses are very similar to those of the Waac,[1] which in turn were patterned after those of the Army men. But the knowing will readily spot certain differences, such as the softer and less-severe design of the nurses' caps.

The Navy Waves and the Marine Corps Women's Reserve, to carry this series of contrasts a bit further, are eligible for officers' commissions—and well-rounded wardrobes—which were beyond the reach of their respective Yeomanette and Marinette predecessors.[2]

In developing the current crop of women's uniforms, the services sought to strike a balance between martial formality and femininity, so a girl could fit into military surroundings, yet not feel irrevocably shorn of all her maidenly graces. To achieve this, they enlisted the aid of accredited designers and stylists—like Mainbocher, who designed the uniforms of the Waves and Spars (Coast Guard). They stressed such disarming objectives as "slenderizing appearance" and "freedom of movement."

[1]WAAC (Women's Army Auxiliary Corps), created in May 1942, was replaced by the WAC (Women's Army Corps) in July 1943.

[2]These terms refer to women during World War I who were in the navy or marines, respectively.

ARMY NURSE CORPS
Field uniform "for service in theater of operations." Note big "cargo" pockets.

NAVY NURSE CORPS
All Navy nurses now have snappy street uniforms, starting rank of ensign.

MARINE CORPS WOMEN'S RESERVE
Model here—Louise Stewart—happens to be bona fide MCWR lieutenant.

WAFS
(Women's Auxiliary Ferrying Squadron)
They have civil-service status, but get same flying suits as Army pilots.

WAAC
(Women's Army Auxiliary Corps)
Uniform of an auxiliary—rank corresponding to private.

ARMY NURSE
(Dress Uniform)
Soon this olive drab will replace the navy blue previously worn by Army nurses.

AWVS
(American Women's Voluntary Service)
One of the most widely seen non-military women's uniforms.

1943
Skirts are shorter, hats are trimmer, shoes are low, uniforms are tailored to the lines of the body. Cosmetics in moderation are approved. Uncle Sam has done his durnedest to show that a girl can simultaneously look feminine and military. One similarity with 1917: most uniforms still include shirt with collar and tie.

RED CROSS
Field Worker in Military and Naval Welfare Service, for soldiers here and abroad.

WAVES
(Women Appointed for Volunteer Emergency Service)
Unlike Yeomanettes, they may get commissions. This is lieutenant, j. g.

FACTORY GUARD
This uniform is unofficial, but appropriate enough, for all that.

On this latter count, the ultimate has probably been reached in a two-piece field slack suit for Army nurses . . . which offers enough movement for a rodeo rider or a steeplejack.

As an all-round testimonial, the epitome may be this unofficial statement by a recently enrolled Wave. "I made up my mind to join," she said, "when I saw that dress uniform. A good two-piece blue suit is one of the most valuable things a girl can own. I can detach the insignia after the war, and get at least three or four years' good wear out of it."

36

VIC HERMAN

"Winnie the WAC" Cartoon
1945

Other indications that the media often portrayed servicewomen in a flippant manner are the cartoons that proliferated featuring either man-crazy

"Isn't he cute?"

hyper-feminine women in uniform or those depicting women as incompetent in their military roles. Corporal Vic Herman's cartoons featuring "Winnie the WAC" appeared in 1,200 army base newspapers, as well as in Life *and* Look. *At times Herman focused on Winnie's shortcomings as a soldier, with one cartoon featuring her at a desk exclaiming, "Goodness, I've put the 12th Armored Division on the Wrong Continent." Others depicted Winnie's interest in attracting male soldiers, as this cartoon illustrates. Although viewers today might see Herman's portrayal of the sexy WAC as demeaning, she was popular among WACs as well as army men at the time.*

37

CHARITY ADAMS EARLEY

One Woman's Army: A Black Officer Remembers the WAC

1989

Fortunately, beyond popular media we can turn to the words of the servicewomen themselves to create a complex sense of who these women were and what they experienced. Charity Adams Earley was the first African American officer in the WAC and would become the highest-ranking black woman in the army. She also commanded the only group of black WACs to serve overseas. They were stationed first in Birmingham, England, then in Rouen, France, and then in Paris. The 6888th was responsible for mail delivery for all American soldiers in Europe. Earley was adamant in fighting racism where she could and providing a congenial environment for her women. In this extract from her memoir, Earley sums up the dilemmas facing black women soldiers and also offers a commentary on army policy toward suspected lesbians.

However routine our activities were for women, it was new to the men to have to make adjustments for and give consideration to female soldiers. As long as we did the job well and we did not interfere with or challenge the maleness of the military, things would go along with surface smoothness.

When Negro women were involved, the situation became slightly more tense. The problems could be summarized as follows:

Charity Adams Earley, *One Woman's Army: A Black Officer Remembers the WAC* (College Station: Texas A&M University Press, 1989), 180–81, 186–87.

The presence of women in the Army was resented by many because traditionally, the military was male.

The resentment was doubled by the service of Negro women because the laws, customs, and mores of the World War II era denigrated and discriminated against Negroes.

Negro males had been systematically degraded and mistreated in the civilian world and the presence of successfully performing Negro women on the scene increased their resentment.

The efforts of the women to be supportive of the men [were] mistaken for competition and patronage.

We lived with these attitudes with dignity. I knew that it was my duty to look out for and protect every member of the 6888th, and I did just that, often assuming the role of the "bad guy" in their eyes. I worked long hours and participated in every activity where my presence could serve the cause. I survived in a state of pleasant belligerency. I had no chip on my shoulder; I kept it slightly below the shoulder. . . .

The chore that was the most difficult for me came in a directive for unit commanders to be alert to homosexual activity. Those of us who came from highly protective backgrounds barely knew what the directive was about and had no idea what to watch for. But we were not stupid, and when there were as many women together as there were in WAC units, attention was always directed at relationships that seemed extra close. When this directive first came to me, I thought long and hard about it. I remembered the childish accusations of misunderstood relationships we heard about in college and in the public arena of work. When I had exhausted my thinking and the discussions with my closest associates, I called the next echelon to ask for guidance in following the directive. The response had two parts: one, the concern should be directed toward those homosexual activities that negatively influenced the performance of the unit, and two, it was suggested that the CO[1] make surprise inspections during the hours when troops were in bed. We had rather an open communication system, so I felt that, had there been any such problem, one of the officers would have heard of it. Besides, we worked hard all day, and I was not about to do a bed check without the company commander, and I was certainly not going to wake up a company commander to accompany me. I cannot swear to the kind of social activity that took place with all the members of the 6888th, but I will swear that the efficient performance of the unit was not impaired.

[1]CO is the shorthand for Commanding Officer.

38

BALTIMORE AFRO-AMERICAN

Four WACs Sentenced to Hard Labor
after Devens Strike

March 24, 1945

*Some black women service members experienced virulent racism
and discrimination. In March 1945, fifty-four black WACS staged
a sit-down strike when on duty at a hospital in Fort Devens in
Massachusetts. This article from the* Baltimore Afro-American
*describes the harsh punishment meted out to four black WACs who
refused to do menial labor that they said was not required of white
WACs. Unlike the Boston NAACP discussed in this article, the national
NAACP sharply criticized the conviction, as did most of the black press.
The following month, after much publicity and complaint from civil
rights activists, the WACs' conviction and sentence to hard labor was
overturned on a technicality and they resumed their duties. Although
the officer responsible for their court-martial was transferred, the army
did not acknowledge the legitimacy of the women's grievances, and little
came from their complaints about discrimination.*

**A thorough War Department Investigation of conditions at the
Lovell Army General Hospital following the convictions and sen-
tencing of four colored WACS after an alleged sitdown strike was
demanded by Congressmen Adam Clayton Powell Jr., and Vito
Marcantonio.**

Fort Devens, Mass. — Four Wacs, convicted on March 20 by a
court-martial board of disobeying a superior officer, were sentenced to
one year at hard labor and ordered dishonorably discharged from the
service.

They were: Pvts. Alice Young, 23, of Washington; Johnnie Murphy, 23,
Rankin, Pa.; Mary E. Green, 21, Conroe, Texas; and Anna C. Morrison,
20, Richmond, Ky., who collapsed when the sentence was pronounced.

"4 Wacs Sentenced to Hard Labor after Devens Strike," *Baltimore Afro-American*, March
24, 1945, 1–2.

The decision, ordered by the board composed of two colored captains, two white Wacs and five other officers, is subject to review by Maj. Sherman Miles of the First Service Command, whose order they disregarded.

The four were among the sixty Wacs who staged a strike last week in protest against alleged discrimination. However, after General Miles read the group the article of war regarding refusal to work, fifty-four returned.[1]

During the two-day hearing, the Wacs contended that their refusal to scrub floors of Lovell General Hospital followed other instances of discrimination on the part of Col. Walter M. Crandall of Vinalhaven, Me., hospital commander.

They charged that he had said that he didn't want "black Wacs"[2] as medical technicians or in the motor pool, adding, "They are here to mop walls, scrub floors and do all the dirty work."

Proof Called Absolute

After the hour's deliberation by the court-martial board, Maj. Leon E. McCarthy of Ansonia, Conn., the trial judge advocate, declared that willful disregarding of the superior officer's order had been proved beyond doubt.

The Wacs were defended by Julian D. Rainey of Boston, a civilian lawyer, who said, "It's a tough thing in this country to be a colored person and subject to discrimination in the face of what we claim to be."

In defense of the girls, he said further that although all they hear is "regardless of race, creed or color," they are told by the officers that they are not wanted for certain duties.

NAACP Disapproval

Earlier, however, the Boston NAACP president, Julian Steele, had issued a statement deploring the action of the Wacs. . . .

It further stated that the Wacs were overly sensitive as a result of the overall policy of segregation in the army, which was termed an underlying but not immediate factor in their case.

---

[1]Recent scholarship indicates that fifty-four women struck but only four continued the strike after being threatened with court-martial.

[2]At the time, most African Americans considered "black" an insulting term.

39

CONCEPCIÓN ESCOBEDO

Oral History Account of a Hispanic WAC
2003

Unlike African Americans, Latino Americans were not segregated in the military. In this oral history, Concepción Escobedo, who was born in Southton, Texas, in 1923 to Mexican American parents, relates her positive experience in the WAC. Her family experienced hard times during the Great Depression and survived on welfare. When her father abandoned the family, Escobedo worked in a department store after school to help support her mother and five sisters. In 1944, at age twenty, she joined the WAC because she could be assigned to Randolph Field, which was near her home in San Antonio. She explained that part of the reason she enlisted was to help her mother and her sisters, who were still in school. She enjoyed her time in the WAC and was able to use the GI bill for further education; she worked most of her adult life. Sandra Freyberg interviewed Escobedo in 2003, when she was eighty years old, for the U.S. Latino & Latina World War II Oral History Project.

Escobedo: They sent me off to basic camp in Fort Oglethorpe, Georgia.... Then they sent me to Randolph Field....

I was always fascinated with the military.... In the school where I went they had R.O.T.C.... I tried out ... I didn't pass.

Freyberg: What did you like about the military?

Escobedo: I liked the discipline. 'Course right away when you go into the service I think you get disciplined twenty-four hours a day and they're very strict.... They yell at you right in front of your face. They had you shaking in your boots. I would get real nervous. But it was only for six weeks.... You had to get up at 5:30....You had to make up your bed. You had chores to do.... You had different duties, like you had to go clean the latrines or maybe sweep or mop, or different things that had to be done. And ... you had to work in the kitchen....

Concepción Escobedo, interview by Sandra Freyberg, September 13, 2003, U.S. Latino & Latina World War II Oral History Project, School of Journalism, University of Texas at Austin. Audio tape transcribed by Lynn Dumenil.

Freyberg: Was there anything that you particularly liked? . . .

Escobedo: Well, I liked the exercise and getting outdoors. I liked the drill, the marching. . . . I just liked that you had to synchronize with the rest of the people. You know you had to . . . be in line, try to keep a straight line. And when there were special occasions, certain days that you would have to go and the higher up officers would want to . . . somebody would come and review the units and we would march in front of them. . . .

Freyberg: Did you have any particular friends there?

Escobedo: . . . No I didn't have any friends. . . . I didn't make any particular friends, you know, just talk to different people. There were mostly Anglos. You know. There were very few and in my unit there weren't any [Mexican Americans?] I don't think. . . .

Freyberg: So, do you think the Anglos accepted you?

Escobedo: Yes. . . . I was never treated badly that I can remember. We were all the same. . . .

Freyberg: After these six weeks of basic training, where did you go?

Escobedo: I went to Randolph Field. . . . When you're in basic, they make you take all kinds of tests to grade you on your ability. . . . They placed me as a file clerk in a file room. And all I had to do was they would bring in papers and we would file them in the correct file. . . . You would rotate I guess the people that worked in the building. And you would have [to] . . . on the weekend answer the phone and you would be the only person in the building, which was very scary because when you're alone and you hear all kind of noises, you know. But it was a good thing that there weren't too many phone calls on the weekend. . . . But I was there only a few months and then there was an opening in the kitchen for a cook's helper, and I always liked the kitchen and so I asked if I could be transferred to the kitchen. I was having trouble with my eyes, getting headaches. . . . And so I went to work as a cook's helper. And later on the baker was transferred from our unit to another place someplace else so I asked if I could be the baker. Could I take the baker's place? And so they approved me and so I was a baker for the squadron, for the women. I don't know how many we were.

Freyberg: What did all the other women do?

Escobedo: They had different jobs. Like when we went to Randolph after basic it was just like having a regular job. Everybody would work.

Like some worked in the motor pool and they were mechanics. Some were drivers for officers. . . . Some were airplane mechanics. Some were secretaries. . . .

The original idea of having women . . . that I knew of was to take the place of a man, do a job that a man was doing so that he could go fight. So he could go to the front lines . . . so women were trying to take the place of men. . . .

Freyberg: Can you remember the reactions from your friends or from the community? . . .

Escobedo: Well, a lot of people didn't like the idea of women going to the service, because of, well, different reasons. Because you would go away from home and it's like anytime you leave home you know you might not—how should I say it—that you won't know how to behave when you're on your own. . . . When I went in in '44 I think . . . there had already been women in the service and people just thought it was not a good idea 'cause you would be messing around with men or whatever.

Freyberg: And did they say something about that? . . .

Escobedo: No. My friends and my neighbors, they thought it was a good idea. I was always kind of an independent person. I've always, most of my life, I've been independent. And so I didn't care what people said. During the war when we would have air raids . . . and I joined to be an air raid warden . . . I would go down the street and make sure everybody turned off their lights. . . .

[Escobedo married right after the war to a man she met on base and moved in with her husband's family.]

They [her husband's family] didn't have a very good opinion of women in the service . . . and they didn't accept me very well. Although they were nice to me but still they were, I kinda had to prove myself . . . that I was a good person . . . not a wild person.

Freyberg: So did women in the army have a wild reputation?

Escobedo: Some of them did. . . . I was accused once of being like the rest of them . . . by my husband's cousin. He said that they knew Wacs and what they were like and I said to him did you see me doing such and such and behaving like that. . . . If you didn't see me, you can't say that I'm just like everybody else. . . .

Freyberg: How did your time in the army change your life? How did it affect you?

Escobedo: I believe that it opened my mind to a lot of things that I saw, because when you live just in a certain area or a certain place where you don't get out anywhere. . . . So when you get out of your own area, your own space, you know, you learn a lot. I learned also because . . . in our families sometimes the mothers are very protective and, you know, they don't tell you a lot of things. Also like in the service they teach you and show you . . . give us information on health and the physics of your body and sex and things like that. In those days, you know, you didn't talk about those things. . . .

[It was good to] learn more about people, learn about yourself, learn how to get along with other people. Because we always lived in a place where mostly Mexican people lived. I didn't have much—except in school—experience with treating Anglos or any other nationality, you know, ethnic groups. When I was in the service, when I was in Randolph Field, a lot of the women that were close to me were from the East, New Jersey, New York . . . northern states. . . .

Freyberg: There was never any discrimination?

Escobedo: No. That I can remember. . . . There were a lot of the women that did not become friends. Some of them would not go past saying just hello. . . . But never to carry on a conversation or anything else to get to know you. That might have been a type of discrimination. I didn't take it as such.

Freyberg: Do you think the war strengthened your position as a woman?

Escobedo: I think it made me—I would say—more worldly.

40

SAN ANTONIO EXPRESS

Fighting Man's Widow Joins Juarez Squadron
March 17, 1944

In March 1944, Mexican American women in Texas were urged to join the newly created Benito Juarez Air WAC Squadron. Named after a nineteenth-century president, the squadron was part of the U.S. Army Air Force, when the Air Force was not yet an independent branch of

"Fighting Man's Widow Joins Juarez Squadron," *San Antonio Express*, March 17, 1944, 1.

service. Texas newspapers, including the Spanish language La Prensa
*(San Antonio), ran frequent appeals to encourage enlistment and also
reported on the large turnout in San Antonio when the squadron as
well as other Air Force WACs were sworn in by WAC leader Oveta Culp
Hobby. The following front-page newspaper article was accompanied by
a photograph of three recruits.*

The youthful, dark-eyed widow of a fighting San Antonian who gave his
life in combat has decided to carry on where her husband left off in the
war against the Axis.[1]

A similar reason prompted Mary Martinez . . . to sign enlistment
papers. Both of her brothers are in action against the Axis. Cpl. Manuel
Martinez is in England, and Seaman Mike Martinez is with the U.S.
Navy.

She [the widow] is Mercedes Ledesma . . . , who this week applied
for membership in the Benito Juarez Air WAC Squadron. With her
when she reported for an interview with A.A.F. officials was her most
cherished possession — a black leather case containing the Purple
Heart Medal awarded posthumously to her husband, Pfc. Domingo
Ledesma. She carries that emblem of supreme sacrifice with her wherever she goes.

One of hundreds of patriotic Latin American men from San Antonio
who have distinguished themselves in battle, Pfc. Ledesma died in the
fighting in Italy.

"I know he would want me to do my part," his widow told Warrant
Officer Charles Treuter when she applied for enlistment. "Both of
us have a lot of friends who're still fighting in Italy — and I think that
trying to help them get back safely to San Antonio is the least any
woman can do."

Among other applicants who are anxious to enter the Benito Juarez
Squadron and help speed the return of San Antonio's "doughboys" are
Alice Vasquez and Freda Rodela, half-sisters. . . . One brother, Corporal
Rodela, is in the army in California, and Pvt. Edward Rodela, another
brother, is serving at Fort Sam Houston.

---

[1]*Axis* was the term used for the alliance between Italy, Germany, and Japan during
World War II.

41

HEART MOUNTAIN SENTINEL

Detachment of Nisei WACs Assigned to Duty at Snelling

November 25, 1944

Around 500 Nisei women served in the WAC during World War II. They were not permitted to enroll until relatively late in the war, after they had signed loyalty oaths. Newspapers put out by inmates at Japanese internment camps praised both the young men and women who served in the military and publicized recruiting efforts. The following account was from one of such internment camp newspapers, Idaho's Heart Mountain Sentinel.

St. Paul Minn. — A detachment of Japanese American WACs, the first WAC [N]isei assigned to duty in Minnesota, has arrived at Fort Snelling.

The chic young women, who look on themselves as soldiers with double duties, are serving at clerical and stenographic tasks, thus relieving the manpower shortage in the school battalion.

They came from different posts around the country and are to be joined later by another contingent of [N]isei WACs now being trained at Fort Des Moines.

The girls, who have smart hair cuts, long, thin polished nails and shoes that gleam, consider themselves double duty soldiers because they not only are doing their part to help win the war.

They are trying desperately by their conduct to correct the misunderstanding many Americans have concerning the [N]isei.

Pfc. Toyme Oyeno, for example, is 22 and pretty. Her father was a section foreman at Pocatello, Idaho. She has a brother in France.

"I joined the WAC to do my part," she said today.

Many of the girls come from farm families. They are quiet, inclined to be shy.

Cpl. Kay Ogura, 22, surgical technician, attended Pasadena junior college. Her father is a landscape gardener. Both her parents are in

---

"Detachment of Nisei WACs Assigned to Duty at Snelling," *Heart Mountain Sentinel*, November 25, 1944, 1.

a relocation center. But she's as gay as any Minnesota girl. She has a brother in France, too.

Never having seen snow falling she's looking forward eagerly to her first Minnesota winter.

Pfc. Bette Nishimura, 25, was a buyer of dresses and shoes for a store at Rocky Ford, Colo. She has what she calls "my kid brother Johnny" in France.

Pfc. Sue Ogata came from Greeley, Colo., where she was a book-keeper. Her brother is at Camp Blanding, Fla.

42

SHAMOKIN NEWS-DISPATCH

Report about WAACs Spiked by Col. Hobby: Refutes Story That Contraceptives Will Be Issued to Auxiliary Members

June 9, 1943

In early June 1943, journalist John O'Donnell claimed that WAACs were to be issued condoms. His story lent fuel to the swirling rumors that military women were sexually immoral. Many newspapers covered the response of Oveta Culp Hobby and other government officials to O'Donnell's story. The United Press account that follows appeared in the Shamokin *(Pennsylvania)* News-Dispatch. *The reference by O'Donnell to "new deal ladies" is a critique of women reformers associated with President Roosevelt's New Deal.*

Colonel Oveta Culp Hobby, director of the Waacs, said today that "there is absolutely no foundation of truth in the statement" that Waacs will be issued contraceptives and prophylactics.

Her statement was in response to inquiries about a column by John O'Donnell of the New York Daily News today which said that such equipment "will be furnished to members of the Waacs according to a super-secret agreement reached by the high ranking officers of the War Department and the Waac chieftan," Mrs. Hobby. . . .

Mrs. Franklin D. Roosevelt told her press conference yesterday, when asked about reports of promiscuity among Waacs, that it was a lot of Nazi propaganda—that naturally the Germans were interested in discrediting an organization which released so many men for the fighting fronts. . . .

Hope Ridings Miller, society page columnist of the Washington Post, wrote recently that "Sex is rearing its vicious head against women-in-uniform. . . . The 'new rumor' hints at evidence of easy virtue in one branch of service particularly."

She then quoted Representative Edith Nourse Rogers, R., Mass., sponsor of the original Waac bill, as saying that time and again such rumors had been reported to her.

"Not once have we found it to be anything but gossip of the most scurrilous sort," Mrs. Rogers said. . . .

O'Donnell, in his column today, said that "health of the girls in uniform and a determined feminine punch to smash through any outmoded standards won the day" in what he said was an agreement to issue contraceptive and prophylactic equipment.

"It was a victory for the new deal ladies," O'Donnell said, "who produced the cold turkey argument that the girls who want to go into uniform and fight what men have called the 'total war' have the same right to indulge their passing fancies."

43

Report of Investigation of WAC Lieutenant for Homosexuality

July 1944

The investigators charged with determining the extent of lesbian activity at Fort Oglethorpe, Georgia, believed that around twenty women at the

Report from Lt. Col. Birge Holt and Capt. Ruby Herman, IGD, to the Acting Inspector General, "Subject: Investigation of conditions in the 3d WAC Training Center," Fort Oglethorpe, Georgia, July 29, 1944, 15–18. Records of the Office of the Inspector General (Record Group 159), National Archives, File 333.9, 3d, Box 17A.

training camp were homosexual. However, they could find little conclusive evidence for either an extensive lesbian network or for explicitly sexual affairs between specific women under investigation. One exception was the case of Lieutenant Patricia L. Warren and Corporal Ruth M. Kellogg, where the committee confronted Warren with letters written between the two women. (It is not clear how these letters were obtained.) Most of the other women investigated indicated that they had been the victims of unwelcome attentions or denied the allegations. The following excerpt is from a summation of the investigation's findings concerning Warren and Kellogg based on the women's testimony, that of witnesses, and copies of the letters.

. . . The two women became acquainted when Cpl. Kellogg was made Platoon Sergeant of Company 11 which Lieut. Warren was commanding. . . . Their acquaintanceship grew to an intimacy which witnesses, during this investigation, testified was obvious. The two women always paired off at social gatherings and were constantly together. . . . During May 1944 Cpl. Kellogg visited Lieut. Warren at Indiantown Gap [Pennsylvania] and spent a two-day pass with her at the Penn Harris Hotel in Harrisburg, Pennsylvania. Cpl. Kellogg stated that she and Lieut. Warren love each other and enjoy each other's company more than that of men. She further testified that she and Lieut. Warren enjoy being close to one another and embracing, but that they have done nothing immoral nor has any perverted act occurred.

. . . A voluminous correspondence between the two women has been carried on since the transfer of Lieut. Warren to Indiantown Gap, Pennsylvania. Two letters written by Lieut. Warren to Cpl. Kellogg were obtained. . . . Both letters are full of love expressions and denote longings, as evidenced by the following sample extract from these letters:

> "Tuesday nite, 6:30 P.M.
> "* * * read your letter for the third time—Honey, it makes me feel so close to you—God, I can feel your arms around me—I can feel your lips covering mine—Aw, Kelly, please come this week end * * *."

* * * * * * *

"Kelly, I love you. I love you so much that I get mad at myself for not being able to find words to express what I am feeling—God, sweetheart, I never would have believed that people could feel what you and I feel for each other. Even though we live the rest of our lives together I will never be able to show you or tell you how very much you mean to me."

* * * * * * *

"I've got you right here with your head on my shoulder and your arms tight around me—and I'm gonna out the light now and lie here and let you hold me and tell me you love me. I worship you, Kelly— I am all yours—I have been since I first found you and I will be forever—* * *."....

... When Cpl. Kellogg appeared before the investigating officers she was told ... of the allegations that indicated an abnormal relationship between her and Lieut. Warren. When asked if she desired to admit these charges or deny them, she answered, "I admit them, sir.". ...

... When Lieut. Warren appeared before the investigating officers she was told ... of the allegations, that she had engaged in an abnormal love affair, such as would normally be expected to occur between a man and woman, and that she had promiscuously associated with an enlisted woman. When asked if there was any statement she cared to make with respect to the charge, she answered:

> "About the only thing I want to do is take all the blame for and clear the kid.". ...

She was then asked:

> "Do you desire to deny or explain to any extent the implications of the language used in the two letters which I have mentioned?"
> to which she replied:

> "It would be utterly impossible to deny it, sir, and as far as I know, I do not think even doctors can explain.". ...

When asked:

> "Have you ever engaged in an affair of this sort with any other woman, Lieutenant?"

Lieut. Warren replied:

> "That is a little unfair question. * * * If we were talking off the record I wouldn't mind answering.". ...

When asked the beginning of the relationship between her and Cpl. Kellogg, Lieut. Warren replied:

> "Colonel, for me to try to tell you the beginning of it, I probably would have to tell you the story of my life, and I know you are not interested in it. I'm willing to admit it; I'm willing to admit it is all my fault. I can't—I just can't see where it would do any good to go into it.". . .

Lieut. Warren expressed conviction that this was an initial experience for Cpl. Kellogg.

[The committee's recommendation was that Lieut. Warren be permitted to resign "For the good of the Service," and that Cpl. Kellogg be hospitalized for psychiatric evaluation and then, depending on whether she could be "reclaimed," either be separated from the army or restored to duty.]

44

ELIZABETH R. POLLOCK

Letters from a WAAC Private to Her Family
1943

An unusual collection of letters from a WAAC undergoing basic training in Des Moines, Iowa, to her family in Philadelphia offers a thoughtful account of her adjustment to army life. Elizabeth R. Pollock could hardly be considered typical. From a prosperous family, she was educated in Europe and trained in the Philadelphia Academy of Fine Arts to become a sculptor. A family member convinced her to publish her letters, and Yes Ma'Am!: The Personal Papers of a WAAC Private *was published in 1943. The following extracts offer her insights as to why she and her colleagues enlisted and an astute assessment of the types of jobs WAACs might be assigned after basic training. Perhaps because of her language skills, Pollock eventually served as a lieutenant in army intelligence in France.*

Elizabeth R. Pollock, *Yes Ma'Am!: The Personal Papers of a WAAC Private* (Philadelphia: J. B. Lippincott Company, 1943), 39–42, 44.

[Pollock seems to be replying to her sister's request for advice about enlisting.]

Dear Sister:

All my life I've been shy about trying to advise anyone, or even influence their actions. I hope the mere fact that I joined up is not what is influencing you. It seems to me that sooner or later, each of us knows what is right for him. It was right for me to enlist, but that has nothing at all to do with you. All I can tell you is what I think and feel — and maybe that will help you decide what your own true feelings are.

I'm really enjoying this experience. It's fun to be among the first and there is a certain amount of excitement in everything we do, even the chores. Day after day I get a lump of emotion in my throat when we stand retreat, or when I see eight hundred women marching in formation. And at night, when we are all talking furiously in the squad-room about the usual things girls talk about, a silence falls when taps sound, and we all lie there, feeling something quite inexpressible far down inside.

Aside from that part of it, which you can probably imagine for yourself, this is in some ways like camp or boarding school or college, only here there is more discipline and team play. At first, of course, it seemed rather silly to have a place for absolutely everything — once my galoshes were at the end of the line of shoes instead of under the bed at the beginning, as the inspecting officer pointed out — but that is part of military discipline, and since then I've seen why discipline is important. I get a little tired, too, now and then, of living with so many people and I thoroughly enjoy walking to the beauty parlor alone. (Under the hair drier [*sic*] is the best place for utter privacy.) The parlor is over past the hospital, near the men's barracks, and there are not so many people about and I enjoy the peace and breathing space to feel myself again. But the psychology of army training, and of girls all working together and sharing the same experiences, is wonderful. I am awfully small and unimportant, of course, but here I feel that what strength I have is being used for a worthwhile purpose.

However, if you think you ought to be doing more than your newspaper work, I think you're wrong. It's quite as important to keep the public alive to what's happening, and since you have a talent for writing, you can probably do it better than the person who would take your place. And some people have to stay civilians to help when the war is over. Don't let yourself be carried away. I should think, if it's adventure you want, there would be more of that after the war, when you can really use your training. Also, it sounds to me as though the WAVES will stay in this country and do clerical work. Evidently WAACs, some of them, at least, will be sent abroad. It is a little difficult to tell you much now, while we're having basic training, because after that is over things will be different. People in the motor corps expect to go overseas, but you know, when you are in the army, if you don't have a specialized training they can use, you are likely to be stuck into a place where there is a crying need for personnel. Here, the last few days, they've been trying to get people for Classification and Drilling, and Cooks and Bakers. . . .

As for myself, I imagine when I get back to Philadelphia I'll be put in Personnel, Intelligence, Operations or Supply. I have a better chance at Personnel or Operations, because I was nearer that before. If I am assigned to Supply, I just hope something in my brain will start clicking. So far our lectures on that subject leave me feeling like a moron!

Noise is beginning again, so I'll have to stop. Just remember that everyone has to go at his own pace! That goes for most decisions in life. Have I told you anything that will help?

Much love, Sister

[In a later letter to her mother, Pollock writes about her fellow enlistees.]
Dear Mother: . . .

Gradually, now, I am getting acquainted with my colleagues. The eighteen girls in my room come from New York, Arizona, Oregon, California, Virginia and Pennsylvania. We are as different as the states we come from, and our pasts are as varied. There is a girl I like especially. Perhaps I have mentioned her before — the one whose husband is missing in the Philippines. She is one of my marching partners and says it's fun to march with me. I can say it is a real pleasure to have her as a pivot when we do column left. Now and then we all talk over our reasons for enlisting. With some, it was because they were separated from their husbands; with others, because they had gotten in a rut in their jobs and wanted to get out. Some of them are like me — they were asked to volunteer because their services were needed in Aircraft Warning. A lot of the girls are happily married, but joined up because they thought there was a job to do. Now that we're here, though, our purposes are all the same. And we all know we're having an experience we shall never forget.

45

MIRIAM E. STEHLIK DRAHOS

Letter Describing Service in North Africa
1943

This letter from the WAC Corporal Miriam E. Stehlik Drahos to an unknown recipient details her dramatic experiences in North Africa. Drahos notes that she works very hard, but does not specify her work, a trend common in letters home as service personnel letters were censored, and they were told not to convey any revealing information about their activities. In Algiers, Drahos was secretary to General (later President) Dwight D. Eisenhower. After the war, she had a career as a secretary in Cedar Rapids, Iowa.

Africa, 1943

Dear—

. . .[1] Now its Africa I'm in! The land of desert sand, cannibals, camels, jungle, and deep mystery. That is what I pictured Africa to be, but so far I have seen nothing but Arabs, Arabs, and more Arabs. They seem to live a very peaceful life. They till their own farms or vineyards with ox and yoke, have no modern equipment, and go right on tending to their own business. Of course the little ones tease you to death begging for "bon bon" and "chawkolat" and "gum chew," for they find that the "Amerikanos" got plenty. I started teaching one of these little urchins to say "What's buzzin cousin"—the best he could do was "What's cousin buzzin." So now all of his little comrades chant it. Every place you turn they want to polish your shoes—claim with American polish!

When we first arrived here, we were given time to get used to our environment and "new home," which was an old French Monastery. Nuns still lived with us, and were very kind. We were told that the little French refugees, for which they are caring, prayed for us each night before we came, so we would arrive safely. In the evenings it was fun to sing and romp with these little girls, for they enjoyed our company a

---

[1]All ellipses in this selection in the original. — Ed.

Alma Lutz, ed., *With Love, Jane: Letters from American Women on the War Fronts* (New York: The John Day Company, 1945), 81–84.

lot, and looked forward to our bringing them candy and gum from our rations.

We will never forget the night of our first air raid! None of us had ever experienced one before, and it was quite a sensation. All of us just lay in our beds, not daring to admit to our "buddies" that we were the least bit afraid, but in our hearts we were trembling. Jerry[2] certainly wanted to give us a royal reception, but then again we wondered why he would want to waste any ammunition on a group of Wacs for they were surely not his objective. After that first initiation, we acclimated ourselves for the ones that followed, for that was all that we could do. I am proud to say that there was not a member in our Company that got hysterical or out of hand. We just took this in our stride, for after all, we knew what we were coming up against.

We are all working now, and long hours. Sunday is just another day to us, as the War won't stop for us to rest on that day. . . . At the end of my working day, I slowly walk home in the gorgeous sunset, knowing in my heart that "paper work" is just as important in this business of war, as is ammunition and supplies — and no day is too long for me to work. I am on the General's staff. . . .

For recreation we have our weekly movies in our Mess Hall, and although some of the pictures are quite old, they are still welcome, and lift us out of GI life for a while. . . . One of the best ways of relaxing is to just go for a long walk down the roads. There you encounter shepherds with their sheep, farmers seated on "itty bitty" donkeys and laden with vegetables and fruits going to the market place, little French boys and girls bidding you "Bonjour Mademoiselle," Arab women with huge baskets of bread on their heads. Then you can stop in any little sidewalk café for a glass of "vino" or champagne! The villages are just a few kilometers apart and it's really interesting to walk from one to another. I spoke of "vino" and champagne; well they flow here like water, but give me a nice cold glass of milk, or a nice chocolate fudge sundae, topped with whipped cream and nuts and a marchino [sic] cherry, and then the French and Arabs could keep it all! . . . .

A lot of our food is in the dehydrated form, such as eggs, potatoes, bully beef, spam, and also we have dried fruits and vegetables. It is amazing how many of the girls now eat bread, that never before have. The Army has its own bakery here, and the bread is really marvelous — so white and soft and fresh!

---

[2]A term for the Germans.

We have been overseas for quite a while now . . . We have gone
without a lot of articles that we thought were absolutely necessary
when we were home, and each and everyone of us has made the
promise that when we get back home again "NONE OF US WILL EVER COM-
PLAIN ABOUT ANYTHING AGAIN."

All of us feel very privileged in being a part of this great North African Campaign, and we know that that is something that no one will ever
be able to take away from us. For in her small way, each of us over here
has helped to write the history of this war, that will be written in books
that our children will read. We are proud to wear that little campaign
ribbon over our left pocket, and when we come marching home again it
will mean more to us than it does now.

Yours for Victory,
"Sunny" (Miriam E. Stehlik)

46

ANNA K. SCHELPER

Letter Describing Nursing in the Philippines

March 8, 1945

---

*This letter was written by army nurse Anna K. Schelper, probably to
her family. Schelper served in a number of South Pacific locales. Here
she describes coming into Manila shortly after the Philippines had been
liberated by U.S. troops. After the war, Schelper made a career in the
army.*

Manila, March 8, 1945

Little did I know, when I last wrote — a month ago, that I'd be where
I am now, and that it would all take place so fast.

The day that I wrote, we received our orders to proceed on an emergency war mission the next day, with no baggage except our hand
bags, limited to fifty pounds. We took off about four in the afternoon

---

Alma Lutz, ed., *With Love, Jane: Letters from American Women on the War Fronts* (New
York: The John Day Company, 1945), 72–75.

and set our feet down at a clearing station three hours later, where we spent the night. All of us, including our own group of nurses as well as a group from a general hospital were given a royal welcome by the corpsmen and officer personnel of this unit, as we were the first female personnel in this section. They didn't like the idea of our staying so near the front lines for the nite, but decided that it was just as safe as to travel by dark.

They fed us first, because they said that there was nothing like a hungry nurse. . . .[1] As the area had not been cleared of mines they sent a soldier to lead the way to the latrine with instructions to keep right behind him, and not stray to either side. Needless to say we did not sleep too soundly that nite, when we were told to go to bed with our clothes on, and discovered that there was a machine gun outside our tent.

About nine A.M. we were loaded onto trucks, with our hand bags on little trailers. To our group had been added a group of picked doctors, including obstetricians, and pediatricians, as well as surgeons. As our convoy traveled down the road, lined with civilians and soldiers, we were so busy trying to see everything, that we didn't feel the sun cooking us, or realize our precarious position. I didn't burn, just got blacker. Of course a thick layer of dust and soot from the flaming city didn't help our appearance.

It was truly a triumphal ride with the amazed, incredulous looks on the faces of the G.I.s when they realized that it was "nurses" they saw, and the Filipinos, from the smallest toddler to toothless old men and women yelling "victory." Most of the road was asphalt, or concrete, with patches of dirt road detours, and an occasional pontoon bridge. It seemed so odd to see buildings, gasoline stations, and civilian clothes again, after all those months in New Guinea. But there was tragedy written on so many faces. There were many people pushing their salvaged household goods along on two-wheeled push carts, or riding in a type of two-wheeled buggy that is peculiar to this region, maybe to find their home in ruins on their return. Hardly a family has not lost a loved one.

It was about two o'clock in the afternoon when our convoy rolled into the grounds of an old school. As we were waiting out in front of one of the buildings, to find out where we were to be quartered, we had time to take in a little of the damage that had been wrought by shell fire, and to notice several rows of new white crosses off to one

---

[1]All ellipses are in the original. — Ed.

side of the road. The nurses who had been on duty here for the past three years could hardly believe their eyes when they saw us, and were told that they were relieved of duty as of that date. They could hardly believe that it could be so soon, as the soldiers had preceded us by only six days. By the time that our trucks had taken us to what had been the girls' dormitory we had all we could do to keep from crying. The trip in had been long and dusty, and we were hungry, but didn't have the face to breath[e] a word about it. So we walked about to see what we could see. . . .

We went to work the next morning, with the 893 Medical Clearing Company, which had set up in this school that has a history of issuing degrees as far back as the seventeenth century, not in these buildings, however. Most of our patients soon came of the civilian class. Every thing you will read, and more is true of the treatment of the Filipinos at the hands of our enemies. Occasionally we'd remind them of the fact that their wounds may have been due to American shells or gunfire but they say that is all right. . . .

Of course, we all worked hard from dawn to dark, with just time enough off every day to take a sponge bath in a helmet of water from an old surface well. Patients didn't often get a bath after the first one on their admission, because the water was scarce, and drinking water precious. However, sometimes we'd use a basin of drinking water for a bath, for the majority of these civilians had been hiding for five to seven days in ditches, or ruins, after they were first wounded, before they'd managed to escape.

One of our girls was on nite duty in the shock ward when she put a small boy on a blanket to sleep in a corner, for he had no place to go. His mother had been brought in as a patient. The nite Sergeant fed the boy soup, the first food he'd had in days. This child then got down on his knees and kissed their hands in gratitude. The climax came when the mother asked the priest to ask them to be the godparents when he baptized him about a week later.

We'd been there about two weeks when the Clearing Company moved out and the Fifth Field Hospital moved in. Things began to quiet down, fewer casualties coming in, and we began to get some sleep, except when sniper fire was too noisy. Our own unit has now moved to a small provincial town near by.

47

HELEN SNAPP

Oral History of a WASP

March 14, 2009

*Helen Snapp was an experienced pilot when she joined the WASPs.
In her oral history, she reports on resistance from male officers and
conveys the commitment of the women pilots. Like other WASPs, Snapp
flew missions that freed up men for combat piloting. These included
towing targets for shooting practice, strafing fake gun installations,
participating in anti-aircraft training, and transporting planes to
various locations.*

[Snapp answers a question about a male colonel.]

He was the one at Camp Davis [North Carolina]. Well, he was a
crusty, up-from-the-ranks officer and . . . he didn't like the idea of the
women being there. . . . He wasn't happy [about a group of twenty-five
women pilots who arrived before her group did], he wouldn't even let
them fly. He wasn't going to have those women flying his airplanes, but
by the time we got there things had simmered down somewhat. I think
he'd been informed that he was going to toe the line. . . . So . . . he was a
little easier on our group. I never had any problems with him.

*[Snapp reports that two women were killed flying at Camp Davis and
responds to the interviewer asking if she had any close calls.]*

Really not so many. The planes were in really bad shape. They were
rejects from the air force, war-weary airplanes. . . . The women turned
down less number of planes than the men did. . . . As long as you realized it was safe to fly for the mission, you went ahead and completed
the mission.

[The interviewer asks about strafing fake gun embankment targets.]

Well, that was so much fun. . . . We were told we didn't have to
go below a certain number of feet but that didn't mean a thing to us.

Helen Snapp interview, The Digital Collections of the National World War II Museum
(2015), Segments 3–4, https://www.ww2online.org/view/helen-snapp. Transcribed by
Lynn Dumenil.

[Laughs] We got as close as we could and people would scatter. And then we'd let our hair fly and let them know it was a woman. . . . I remember being mooned once! . . .

[Snapp discusses the end of the WASP program.]

We were all discharged at the same time the WASPs at all the bases in December of '44. . . .

[She responds to a question about her thoughts upon hearing about the cancellation of the program.]

Well, we were supposed to be militarized, that was the worst of it. [There was discussion of converting the WASPs from civilian to military status.] . . . And there was some dispute about who was going to be in charge of it, [WASP director Jacqueline] Cochran or they were going to put us in the WACs. And we were a little nervous about that whole situation anyway. . . . We were told that it didn't mean we would end up flying so I wasn't actually for it at that time anyway because if we ended up with the WACs or ended up in the air force in non-flying jobs and that's what we were in there for, was flying. So it never happened anyway and it fell through. And even though we took officers' training courses and took the same training that the men did, it didn't happen. . . . Some of 'em [her colleagues] were gung ho anyway, they said would fly free and wrote to everyone they could think of and some were so disappointed because they had left good jobs to get into the air force . . . and it wasn't that easy to return to civilian life once you had been doing that so it was pretty hard on some people. . . . It was so hard on the women because if a woman died in the service, in the WASPs, she had no benefits whatsoever. Actually Cochran paid for some of the women to be shipped back and a WASP was assigned to go with the casket back to the home. . . .

Our pay continued to be much less than the men did. [*sic*] It wasn't the pay so much—we were happy with what we were doing—it was the fact that we didn't have any benefits. . . . Some of the women who had service-connected disabilities had no recourse. In the seventies that was rectified and we did get veteran status [granted by Congress in 1977].

6

The End of the War and Beyond

Even before the war in Europe ended in May 1945, government officials, employers, and the media began to question what would happen to women's jobs when servicemen came home. Although the Women's Bureau survey indicated that 75 percent of those working in ten defense plants wanted to keep their jobs, and many union activists, too, insisted that women had earned their place in a wide range of industrial jobs, women were laid off in massive numbers, with little attention paid to their job seniority in relation to civilian men. Women were fired at a rate 75 percent higher than men. The documents presented here explore the debate over women's proper roles as the war came to an end. While many of the attitudes reflected traditional roles for women as homemakers, others, including Women's Bureau leaders and union activists, proposed a permanent role for women in the workforce. In what ways do these documents express traditional notions about women's role in the family, and in what ways do they challenge it? To what extent can we see feminist strivings for equality between men and women?

48

CATHERINE HAMBLEY

Asserts Women Be Given Chance in Postwar Era
March 15, 1945

As the war ended, newspapers and magazines reported extensively on the dilemmas facing working women who experienced widespread unemployment as war contracts wound down. They drew heavily upon

Catherine Hambley, "Asserts Women Be Given Chance in Postwar Era," *Evening Star* (Washington, D.C.), March 15, 1945, 21.

surveys and reports from the Women's Bureau, which sought to explain
that women were not temporary members of the workforce and that they
deserved equity and fair pay in the labor market. In the excerpt below,
published in the Washington, D.C., Evening Star, *reporter Catherine*
Hambley summarizes a speech by Women's Bureau head Frieda Miller.
Note that Miller challenges notions about women's experiences in the
workplace, but also seems to accept prevailing ideas about appropriate
women's work.

The Nation's social and economic structure will suffer if job opportunities are not kept open in the postwar era for millions of gainfully employed women, Frieda S. Miller, chief of the Women's Division, Department of Labor, declared yesterday.

Speaking at a combined luncheon meeting of the Soroptimist Club[1] and the Women's Advertising Club, Miss Miller pointed out that in 1944 there were 18,500,000 women employed, with 500,000 looking for work. In contrast, 11,000,000 women were employed in 1940, with 2,500,000 seeking employment. About one-half of the newcomers in the commercial field were formerly occupied in homes, she explained, while one-third are young people who had never worked before.

According to a survey, approximately 80 per cent of the total number now hired wish to continue working after the close of hostilities, the speaker said.

She warned that workers who must seek gainful employment because they have obligations either to themselves or to dependents must be given the chance through full employment to compete in the job market. Otherwise, the country will resort to public relief or to the old system whereby "old maids" became the responsibility of their kin.

Trained workers with special skills who have stuck by their professions will be in the more stable postwar position, Miss Miller asserted. Workers, particularly those who have moved into spheres formerly occupied only by men, such as in heavy industries, may have to shift into work areas such as the service industries, she added. These labor areas, the division chief declared, should be made more attractive to

[1]Soroptimist International, founded in 1921, is a service club for women interested in improving the lives of women and girls.

them and should offer decent and satisfactory employment conditions. New occupations, such as the ever-increasing health and nutrition services, will open new avenues of opportunities for women.

The speaker advised women against accepting jobs for less pay than that received by men. An advocate of equal pay for equal work, she condemned the unequal policy as short-sighted, adding that in the long run it only accomplished pulling down wage levels.

49

MARJORIE McKENZIE

Pursuit of Democracy
September 8, 1945

The mainstream media rarely addressed the problems faced by black women in the postwar labor market. Black magazines and newspapers covered African American unemployment issues, but did not especially focus on women. This article by Marjorie McKenzie is an exception. It appeared in the African American newspaper the Pittsburgh Courier.

The most disgruntled group of victory workers of the entire war effort, the ladies who unwillingly got acquainted with the decor of their own kitchens, are making some quiet peace plans of their own. They have their sights well aimed on the thousands of Negro women who are currently unemployed as the result of munitions cutbacks. Perhaps no pre-war employer class is as ready with full employment offers as this one.[1] Furthermore, it wants to put the industry [meaning paid household labor] back on the old basis with no retooling, reorganization, nor increased overhead contemplated.

It goes without saying that these eager, would-be employers, who with their prospective employees have hit the reconversion market earlier than anyone else, have plenty of support. Unwittingly (in some instances) help is chiefly coming from the United States Employment

---

[1]McKenzie is suggesting here, sarcastically, that women eager to hire domestic servants are a group willing to offer "full employment."

Marjorie McKenzie, "Pursuit of Democracy," *Pittsburgh Courier*, September 8, 1945, 7.

offices, where Negro women war workers are filing claims for unemployment compensation and seeking re-employment. The payment of compensation is, of course, dependent upon continued unemployment and the assumption that the applicant is able to work and actively looking for it. If the employment office is able to offer the applicant a job for which she has the qualifications of previous experience, she is bound either to accept or to forego compensation benefits.

Large-scale industrial employment for Negro women is almost wholly a war-time phenomenon. In 1940, a little over 1.5 million Negro women were in the labor force. By April 1944, the female labor force had increased to 2.1 million, an additional 600,000 workers. The most significant occupational shift was from the farm to the factory. Although the proportionate distribution of Negro women in the unskilled jobs did not improve, the actual number employed as factory workers was four times greater. They made important contributions at all skill levels in shipyards, aircraft plants, in electrical equipment and machinery, in ordnance and in steel mills, especially foundries. Their war-supporting activities in civilian industry such as laundries, restaurants, canneries and in transportation and textiles offered new occupation opportunities.

These women, accustomed to an impersonal employer, controlled working conditions, the protection of labor organizations and to higher wages and shorter hours than are characteristic of domestic employment, will not want to return readily to their former work. It may be all that they knew before obtaining war training and employment, but the work situation of a domestic does not thereby become any more acceptable to them as a post-war way of life. Whether they should be required to accept it when they apply for the substantial compensation that, based on their war wages, would be theirs, is an urgent question which social planners must answer immediately. If one large segment of the war labor force is forced back to pre-war levels of under employment, the first step in a downward spiral of limited consumer power, overproduction and ultimate depression is taken.

We can maintain prosperity only by utilizing all persons who want to work at the highest levels of skill and at wages which preserve their ability to buy the goods they need for a decent standard of living.

It is not necessary to sacrifice Negro women workers to the maintenance of American homes. American ingenuity is already at work developing commercial cleaning, cooking and laundry services which will be cheaper and more efficient than the efforts of unwilling household drudges.

50

BARBARA WOOLLCOTT

We Want Our Jobs
March 4, 1945

In addition to addressing the dilemma that working women faced in the context of widespread unemployment, the media also occasionally ran articles that were clearly feminist in tone, ones that questioned women's exclusive role in the home in the wake of the war. The following essay, written by Barbara Woollcott, appeared in the Los Angeles Times *and is outspoken in calling for rethinking women's work lives.*

We've been hearing all kinds of talk, lately, about getting women to go back where they came from. A year ago, it was the question, "How can we prod them out of their kitchens and put them to work in vital war industries?" Now certain uneasy males begin to hold forth on ways and means of reversing the process.

That women will go back to their prewar occupations, that they must go back, seems to be a foregone conclusion. No problem there. But, we are informed dolefully, women have changed. The former housewife's horizon has been broadened by work done and contacts made during this war period. How can we persuade her that true contentment lies only within the four walls of her home? How can we "readjust" her so that she will be happy — or at least docile — in her old way of life?

Frankly, I don't think we can.

Table-talk Experts

The "readjustment" talk emanates largely from professors, writers of editorials, and table-talk experts. I worked in a Detroit war plant for a year and a half, and among my friends and fellow workers there, I do not believe I ever heard this issue raised.

Not that the girls weren't given to discussions. They were. But it was not a question of readjustment. It was, simply, as it was with the men, "How can we hold our jobs?"

Barbara Woollcott, "We Want Our Jobs," *Los Angeles Times*, March 4, 1945, F9.

Some of the men felt that women should go on working if they wanted to. Others thought not.

"My wife isn't going to work after the war, you can bet on that. She'll stay at home to look after the kids or else!"

Just like that—the "knock-'em-down-and-drag-'em-home" method. A shade less subtle and delicate than the "ease-them-back-and-readjust-them" school of thought. Doubtless, one will be about as effective as the other.

For it is how the women feel that will be decisive.

Some women, naturally, are eager to be housewives again. They will be happy to take up where they left off.

I certainly don't intend to imply that they are any less admirable for preferring housework. But why assume that this is the preference of all women? Or that if it isn't, they will have to do it anyhow? This seems about as absurd as decreeing that all men must be public accountants, regardless of their desires, talents and training.

There are a great many women who want to go on working at their present jobs after the war ends. All kinds of women—married and unmarried, young and old, women with special talents and women who are just capable average workers.

We often hear that women will have to give up their jobs to returning servicemen. Well, I don't know any women who want to hold jobs at the expense of our veterans. But then, I don't know any men who do either. As I heard one man in our plant comment: "The day a discharged soldier walks in here and asks for a job, I'm willing to pack up my tool box and let him have my place."

It was a fine thing to say; and he meant it. Yet no one suggests that we assure veterans jobs by throwing men in factories out of work. We have been planning jobs for present workers and returning soldiers alike. I do not know why the same constructive attitude can't be taken toward women who want to keep on working.

Women today take their jobs seriously, and for the same reason men do.

Must Make a Living

The all-important reason, of course, is to make a living. Some need to work because their husbands are in the Army, and they cannot get along on a soldier's pay. And when the war ends, there are husbands who won't be coming back. Some who do return will not be able to work for a while. A few may never be able to work again. For their wives, jobs will be a necessity.

Women who are not married will certainly have to support themselves. And it is generally agreed that this generation will have more than its share of single women, with the war's taking its toll of our young men.

Many married women, too, will want to keep on working because of economic pressure. People who have long needed medical and dental care are finally able to afford it. Couples have bought homes because they were making enough money to meet payments; and they count on two pay checks to help them continue after the war.

Besides, a lot of women have found their jobs more interesting, more stimulating, and above all more social, than housework. There are certainly very few men who would enjoy staying home all day, even if they could afford it. . . .

Continue Day Nurseries

Some people point out that women who hold jobs do so at the expense of having children, and that if women continue to work, the birth rate will decline. But would this be so if conditions were made easier for working mothers? If day nurseries, started during the war to help them, could continue and increase; if regular leaves-of-absence could be arranged for pregnant women; if perhaps some system of a shorter day could be managed for women who must work but who also have homes and families to take care of? Under such circumstances women with the additional financial security of a job might be more eager to have children than non-working wives are.

Wife's Tired Too

In many cases it has been possible for women to work during the war because of help given them by family and neighbors. Many a husband has taken on household duties, realizing that his wife, too, was tired after a full day's work. Many children have taken on their share of work, or have assumed responsibility in the care of younger children. Neighbors have shared cars to finish a week's shopping in a single evening, asked children next door in to lunch because their mother was at work.

Maybe something was gained here beyond the immediate objective. A better understanding between husband and wife, greater responsibility on the part of children, a deeper community sense in big cities where once next-door neighbors never spoke to each other. We have discovered something good; let's not lose it.

Some say, "But it won't work, once the war ends." The same ones, no doubt, who said that women could never be trained for the work they are now doing.

Can America be as resourceful and energetic in its peacetime program as it has been in its wartime program? If so, the skeptics will be wrong again.

51

BERNICE MORGAN

Women War Workers Shun Domesticity

August 19, 1945

In addition to general articles featuring the debate over working women after the war, the media also explored the personal angle by publishing interviews with women about their postwar plans. The following document is typical of those that indicated women's interest in keeping their current jobs. The article is unique in mentioning a Nisei woman, Helen Osada, who came to Rochester, New York, looking for secretarial work after her release from a Japanese internment camp in Arizona. Osada was twenty-two at the time and had some college experience. Her government relocation records reveal that she had worked as a farmhand and in clerical work.

Now 9,000 women war workers laid off in Rochester in the last week know how Cinderella felt—for the era of golden economic equality in which they dwelt for three years has turned into a pumpkin.

Unlike Cinderella, however, most of them aren't going to sit by the fire, or even in the kitchen, if they have anything to say about it.

Lured into the industrial world by high wages, the former woman war worker isn't snapping up offers of jobs as a waitress, maid or housekeeper. She came into her own once, doing men's work at men's pay rates, and she hopes to stay there.

Nobody wants to discourage her, but the facts as revealed by Area War Manpower Commission Director Russell C. McCarthy indicate

Bernice Morgan, "Women War Workers Shun Domesticity; Most of Those Laid Off Hunt New Jobs," *Democrat and Chronicle* (Rochester, New York), August 19, 1945, 19.

that the average laid-off woman war worker's belief that she'll be back in a comparable job at comparable pay within a few weeks when reconversion is under way is wrong.

Most of the women were on light assembly work and single operation machine work — and when war contracts ended those jobs for women were permanently terminated also. The majority of such workers will find plenty of jobs available, but not in the work and at the rates they have been pulling down.

A survey yesterday indicated that approximately two-thirds, or 6,000 of those terminated up to date, plan to continue working despite the fact that total victory is here.

Enjoy New Independence

The reason? They like their new-found independence. But questioning shows that for many of them the reasons go deeper than that — they say they have to earn their own living or must support others.

White-haired Mrs. Clarence Raymond . . . , a 51-year-old erstwhile housewife who went into war work three years ago and was laid off Monday by the General Railway Signal Company said:

"I'm honestly not crazy about the heavy work I was doing. Handling and packing 105 mm. shells that weigh 29 pounds apiece is no picnic. But I've got to keep working. My two sons are still overseas, my husband isn't very well, although he is still working. I'd rather stay home, but I've got to plan ahead."

Know Legal Benefits

They know their legal benefits. For instance, they're shopping around, not taking the first offers in the many service jobs being described to them. They are, in fact, taking the $21 a week unemployment insurance benefit (or as much of it as they are entitled to) and looking around.

Friday there were 1,400 job applicants [in Rochester], 65 per cent of whom — or 910 — were women. . . .

One look is evidence enough that these women are nothing like the downtrodden job seekers of the depression. Well-groomed, in fresh, summery dresses, they are a far cry from the slack-clad women who have been forging the weapons of war to bring the nation to victory.

The ones who are most willing to quit are former housewives who entered industry during the war. Former school girls, who have known no work but war work don't even consider quitting.

The youngsters, who have been pulling down top wages during the war, are probably headed for an era of disillusionment. Openly woeful yesterday was 16-year-old Helen Guck. . . . Pretty, brunette Helen, still in her teens, grew up in an age of plenty of jobs, plenty of money. She was earning $30 a week for a 48-hour week when she was laid off Friday. Helen, who assembled parts on the tail system and control boxes for B-25 bombers, has been working a year.

"I think I'll be back in the factory, where I like it best," she said. "They said they expect to call us in."

Shun Housework

Although none of the women questioned has plans for training in new lines of work, such as beauty culture, nursing, returning to school or stenography, they are all unanimously agreed in their answer to one question—NO. They do not want to do housework!

Mrs. Helen E. Starke, . . . who was in charge of final inspection of shells for the F.A. Smith Manufacturing Company, expressed the sentiments of many when she said, "I don't want to be somebody's servant. I've kept house most of my life for my husband and children. In fact, it's all I ever did before entering war work a few years ago.". . .

Most of the women interviewed don't believe that women get enough pay in civilian lines. They figure $35 a week as a decent wage, with the clerical workers considering $30 to be "good."

Christine Stulpin, . . . whose take-home pay for a 45-hour week at F.H. Smith average[d] $35, said, "Women work just as hard as men. Why should they be asked to take less money?". . .

Probably the most startled person in the city at the impact of the mass layoffs was Helen Osada, a 21-year-old Japanese-American of Suisan, Calif., who came into the city yesterday from the Gila River Relocation Center in Arizona. Helen probably picked the worst day in history to look for a job, but she didn't want to waste any time. A skilled stenographer, . . . she said, "I wanted to be a secretary, but I'm not so sure I'll ever make it when I look around at all these other girls in the same boat. And they've lived here most of their lives, too!" . . .

[The final comment about women's desire to continue working came from Ann Macksamie.]

"I don't know what I'd do if I couldn't work for a living."

52

SEATTLE DAILY TIMES

Most Women Workers Plan to Give Up Jobs after War

December 25, 1944

In contrast to the previous newspaper report, in December 1944 the
Seattle Daily Times *ran an article entitled, "Most Women Workers Plan
to Give Up Jobs after War." Note the contradiction between the headline
and the inclusion of women who clearly intended to work after the war.
It is also useful to realize that the* Times *did not just interview women
in defense industry jobs, where women were pulling down good wages.*

Most of the women working in the Seattle war plants will be more than
willing to let returning service men take back their old jobs after the
war, it was indicated in a survey conducted among the women workers.

The majority of the women questioned—picked at random while on
the job—still felt that "woman's place is in the home."

"I'm not going to work, I know that," said Nora DeWitt, . . . a
machine operator at the American Can Company plant. "I think most of
the girls plan to stay home and raise families, at least that's what they
are saying—and that's about all they talk about. Most of them will be
happy to hand their jobs over to their husbands.". . .

Miss Lois Lang, . . . employed as a meat cutter said:

Jobs Should Go to Men

"If the women workers are still needed after the war, they should keep
on working. Otherwise, the jobs should go back to the men. I've been
in the meat-cutting business for three years, but the minute the men
butchers get back I'm getting out.". . .

Mrs. Charles B. McSwain, . . . employed on the service floor of a tire
shop, said she had settled the question in her own mind a long time ago.

"A woman who really is holding a man's job should relinquish that job
after the war, especially if she is a married woman," said Mrs. McSwain.

"Most Women Workers Plan to Give Up Jobs after War," *Seattle Daily Times*, December
25, 1944, II-13.

Mrs. Lee Burtt, . . . head checker in a chain grocery store, feels the situation depends on the women themselves.

"If women want to stay in industry they should be able to," she said. "Of course, a lot won't want to. I don't know whether I'll be working then or not." . . .

Lilas Wilford, . . . a slitter at the can company plant, believes women will be needed a long time yet.

"Until the service men are returned to private life the women of the country will be needed in industry," she said. "As for myself, I'm a widow and will have to work. However, I'm sure that most of the girls are only waiting for the war to end and for their men folks to come home for a chance to quit working."

Dorothy Porrier, . . . a packer at the can company plant, intends to keep on working.

"I like the independence and income I derive from working," she explained. "I have a boy friend in the South Pacific, but I don't want to get married right now. I don't know what he thinks about it."

53

ELIZABETH JANEWAY

Meet a Demobilized Housewife
November 1945

In yet another version of women's return to domesticity, a Ladies Home Journal *article, "Meet a Demobilized Housewife," offered a detailed account of Ruth Tillson, who had worked on submarines, but was now happy to have returned to her home and family, which consisted of her husband, Rusty, who was intermittently away on military service, and a baby. But the article also suggests this transition is fraught with other complications.*

"Here's the formula," Ruth said. "Bye-bye, Gerry. Be a good girl. See you later." Gerry looked after her mother thoughtfully, but Ruth

Elizabeth Janeway, "Meet a Demobilized Housewife," *Ladies Home Journal* 62 (November 1945): 158–59, 170.

didn't turn back. *She's perfectly all right with Mrs. Akrigg,* she thought. *Mrs. Akrigg looks after lots of children—she had eleven last month. She's licensed by the state. She thinks Gerry's sweet. This won't be for always, and anyway, I'll get used to leaving her sometime.* She went on to the bus stop. The six-o'clock bus was due in two minutes. . . .

She got off into another world. The gates of the Electric Boat Company, biggest makers of submarines in America, were lit brightly from overhead, and the guards stood checking badges as the day shift arrived. Ruth (No. 1950) punched in, pushed through the gates and down to the cafeteria. . . . Then in the locker room she pulled on her leather trousers and jacket, tucked her crisp dark hair under a helmet, and picked up her gloves and mask. When these were adjusted there was no trace left of Mrs. R. W. Tillson, housewife. For the next five hours, with one fifteen-minute rest period, she would make the sparks fly and the air hum. Ruth had become part of America's sudden new creative response to war, part of the unpredictable secret of production that our enemies had never imagined possible. She was a welder, a builder of submarines, good enough and experienced enough to work on the ways[1] with the men. In 1944, the year just past, the Electric Boat Company had delivered twenty-seven submarines to the Government.

Thousands of women made that record possible. Many of them, like Ruth, worked too hard, slept too little, ate on the run, and when the final whistle blew came home to stacks of clothes to be washed, floors to be scrubbed, hungry people to be fed. The weariness and strain in their faces were not paid for by the money they made, and the mark on their spirits was as real as any foxhole fatigues. These war heroes' wages were only collected last summer—victory, the end of the war and the men coming back. . . .

But when Ruth stopped working, her $51 a week stopped too, Rusty had received a promotion to boatswain's mate 1st class, with a salary of $144 a month instead of $96. But food and other necessities have kept going up and getting harder to find and money has become a constant gnawing threat.

Then there is the problem of the future. Rusty's discharge from the Navy will come six months after the end of the war. He enlisted in the regular Navy, not in the reserves, and he can re-enlist and stay if he wants to. Ruth wants him to. The economic security the Navy offers means a lot to her.

---

[1]"The ways" refers to the site where ships are under construction.

But Rusty doesn't see how they could have anything but the barest, meanest life on Navy pay, secure as it is. . . . Suppose he goes back to boatswain's mate 2nd class and $96 a month, with no family allotment? How can you keep a wife and kids on that?

54

BEATRICE BERG

When GI Girls Return
April 22, 1945

As they did with civilian women, newspapers and magazines addressed the question of the postwar future of women in uniform. And, as was often the case with accounts of civilian defense workers, authors often seemed to contradict themselves. In this 1945 article, columnist Beatrice Berg cites a survey, without detailing its nature, and argues both that service women can't wait to return to home and family and that many are eager to use their military training for careers.

When the Wacs, the Waves, the Spars and the lady Marines were first added to our armed forces, opponents to women in uniform raised the bugaboo that the women of America would come out of uniform barking like drill sergeants They won't be fit companions for civilian men, they'll never settle down to being wives and mothers, and their morals—the arguments would end at this point with a sorrowful shaking of the head.

A survey of Woman's Army Corps members stationed in the New York area indicates that all this headshaking was unnecessary. Being in uniform has not deprived them of their essential femininity nor their normal desires for husband, home and children. On the contrary it has in many instances convinced the "By God, I'm going to be a career woman" girls that marriage is not only a sacrament but something they might be interested in when the boys come home.

Beatrice Berg, "When GI Girls Return," *New York Times*, April 22, 1945, SM21.

Their experience in the services, most uniformed girls report, has helped them see more clearly woman's place in the general scheme of things. They don't feel that life is a struggle between the sexes for supremacy, nor do they think that women are going to try to run the post-war world. However, they do believe they have extended feminine horizons by proving that women could make important contribution in wartime, and peacetime, too.

Wac Lieut. Irma Bouton, who served nine months in North Africa as a noncommissioned officer, is typical of the majority of women in uniform. Her one and only post-war plan is to get married. She has the bridegroom already picked out and the only barrier between her and the altar is the 5,000 miles that separate her and her future husband.

"So far as I'm concerned," said Lieutenant Bouton, "men are still the guys who bring home the bacon. One thing I've learned in the Army is to appreciate the simpler things in life. When I get out I want to have a home and enjoy those simple things.

Another thing I've learned is confidence in myself. In the Wac a job is thrown at you, and it is assumed that you can do it. I've had some pretty tough assignments, but I've had to do them. That does something to you; pretty soon you aren't afraid of anything. I think that will make me a better homemaker."

Those girls who plan to combine marriage and a job talk in terms of working "just for a few years." Some of them are worried about whether their husbands and sweethearts will be able to get jobs when they get back from overseas, and they anticipate having to work for a while to help out.

It is estimated that only 25 per cent of returning service men will want to go back to their pre-war jobs, and it seems probable that even fewer service women will resume their peacetime chores. Girls who held routine clerical jobs or worked as salesgirls or in beauty shops, and even some professional women, have acquired new skills and new ambitions.

Wac Lieut. Madeline Bushman, who used to teach physical education, has had just such an experience. "The Army has taught me things about myself I never knew before," she said. "When I returned from North Africa I was asked to give some radio talks. I was terrified and tried to get out of it. But I gave the talks and the more radio work I did, the more I loved it. Now I think I'd scrub floors in a radio station for the chance to do some acting or announcing. I'm certainly not going back to teaching physical education if I can help it."

Girls who held interesting jobs before the war summoned them to temporarily more important tasks are for the most part planning to pick up where they left off. And those who were in school and college are generally planning to take advantage of the educational provisions of the GI Bill of Rights.[1]

And, strange as it may seem, there are many service women who would like nothing better than to remain in uniform if the women's services are continued as a permanent part of our armed forces. They find some encouragement in the announcement by Representative E. E. Cox of Georgia that he would seek a commission to study plans for a military academy for women officers. Pfc. Thelma Giddings, a member of the Negro detachment at Halloran General Hospital, is representative of this group.

"They're just going to have to kick me out of this Army," said Thelma, who was a domestic before the war but who has become a surgical technician in the Army. "Ever since I was a little girl I wanted to be a soldier. The Wac was made to order for me. I sure would like to stay in after the war."

[1]The Servicemen's Readjustment Act of 1944 provided benefits such as education subsidies and home loans to World War II veterans.

55

THERESE BENEDEK

Marital Breakers Ahead?
September 1945

Although many newspapers and magazines sought to examine the working woman issue through the eyes of women themselves, the discussion was often linked to examining the expectations of men in the postwar era. Articles urged women to be attuned to the emotional state of returned veterans and not to let their wartime experience of independence undermine men's desire to return to conventional family life. The following article, written by psychologist Therese Benedek,

Therese Benedek, "Marital Breakers Ahead?" *Parents Magazine* 20 (September 1945): 32, 149–51.

appeared in Parents Magazine. *It acknowledged men's responsibilities in sustaining marriage, but focused primarily on women's obligations. The extract here specifically addressed the dilemmas faced by women who worked during the war. It reflects the persistent call for women and men to adhere to traditional gender roles as a means of achieving social order, a theme that characterized much of mainstream culture in the decade after the war.*

Keeping a family together and preparing a welcoming home for her returning soldier is an extremely grave responsibility for any woman. The task is even more difficult since it cannot be achieved solely by good intentions. It is not enough just to keep up the home, not enough just to want to reestablish the marriage. The soldier has been without love for too long and therefore, he will need it more than ever. . . . He will need many signs of real love, emotional understanding, until he finds that his home is a place to relax in. . . .

Fortunately, there are many women who make good adjustments to separation, who know how to wait and not become embittered. . . . But they too have problems which they have to face, during the remaining period of wartime separation, and also, when their husbands return home.

These women took separation in their stride and many carried on their husbands' work. This is probably especially true for wives on farms and wives of small business men. They stepped into the business and filled their husbands' places. In the big cities and in towns with war plants, many women went to work for the first time outside of the home. Are they satisfied? Sometimes they are not only satisfied, but proud. They are generally profiting from the boom; they often earn more money than they ever saw before; they can buy things for themselves, or for their homes or their future homes, which they had only dreamed about before. However, many of these women foresee conflicts which may grow out of their increasing independence. Will they like giving up work and going home to be housewives when their husbands return? Will they be satisfied when they have to ask their husbands for money after they have been used to earning it themselves? Such a woman has conflicting wishes. On the one hand, she wants to have a husband, satisfied, and happy in his own achievement, but on the other, she is aware of the satisfactions that come from work and independence. Many a woman asks herself, "How will this affect my husband? Will he like it? Will I like it if he does not appreciate my work or does not think it is important?" We find many women seeking answers to these questions. The answers are different, depending not only on the wife and on her desire for work, but also upon her husband's attitude toward economic independence for women in general, and the independence of his own wife in particular. It is interesting to observe how sensitively some women can measure the degree of independence and growth their husbands will be able to accept without conflict.

Many men sound very proud when they tell what their wives are able to accomplish — household, children, earning a wage and all. But many of the soldiers say, "That is only until I get home." [The statement often] . . . does not express sympathy for the wife but fear of her, since her capacity to be self-sufficient seems to threaten his position in the family and shakes his belief in his own masculinity.

Wives may gladly give up their hard-earned independence if their husbands are able to fulfill their needs emotionally and otherwise; but it may be impossible and they may be thoroughly resentful if they feel that their husbands' demand is based not on strength and love but on fear and insecurity.

Wives should realize that some of the insecurities and fears of the returning soldier do not represent innate weakness, but are created by a special situation. . . . When he becomes a civilian again the measure of masculinity is completely different; overseas stripes and campaign ribbons are not enough; he will want to reestablish himself as the provider and head of the family. He may, however, encounter difficulties. He may find civilian competition very hard to take and he may resent his working wife and all women who have jobs. . . . He may demand that his wife give up all outside work and devote herself to the care of the house and children.

Many women will gladly do this. Young women who have babies after their husband's return will have a natural need to stay at home. The pregnancy, the care of the infant, will facilitate the wife's adjustment to home and husband as it will facilitate the veteran's adjustment to family life. . . . The satisfaction of parenthood not only reestablishes his feelings of masculinity but gives his wife a permissible, biological reason for indulging a dependence most women enjoy. . . . Thus, the common experience of parenthood will give both husband and wife not only the time but also the willingness to learn again each other's habits and wishes, strengths and weaknesses; they will find new solutions for their problems including, perhaps the wife's desire for independent work. . . .

Knowing that marriage with a veteran is a job and not a simple realization of fantasies will help both husbands and wives to overcome the difficulties which result from the fact that they have lived such an important period of their lives apart.

Will they be like strangers? Yes, they may well meet again as strangers if there are not important experiences which can bridge the distance between them. But love and sexual attraction, the experience which their marriage represents, are powerful allies in overcoming the estrangement created by the war and in winning peace and happiness in marriage.

56

NEW YORK TIMES

UAW Women Workers' Protest of Layoffs at Ford Motor Company
November 8, 1945

Perhaps the most vehement supporters of women's rights to work and to work at good jobs and fair pay came from union women. As they faced layoffs, women activists focused especially on the issue of seniority, a union principle built into contracts that required employers to fire and hire based on an employee's length of service. However, when companies began mass layoffs in 1945, they largely ignored women's claims to seniority. Although relatively few male unionists were willing to support women's claims to fair treatment, in Detroit UAW women successfully pressured men to support them in their complaints against management. In the following article, the New York Times *reported on the November 1945 picket line that UAW women organized to protest Ford's refusal to acknowledge their seniority rights when it began rehiring workers for tractor production. The protest failed, but their militancy foreshadowed union women's persistence in carving out better opportunities for working women in the postwar decades.*

"A Complaint from the Women," *New York Times*, November 9, 1945, 12.

DETROIT, Nov. 8—Waving placards which proclaimed that "the hand that rocked the cradle can build tractors, too," about 150 women, displaced from their wartime jobs, threw up a picket line today at the Highland Park plant of the Ford Motor Company.

The women, carrying other signs which told male workers that their seniority was not safe, either, and protesting alleged discrimination against female workers, said that they would remain on the picket line until their seniority rights were restored.

They established the picket line, they said, after they had been laid off and their jobs taken by new male employes without seniority.

Ford officials said that the women were not being hired at the plant at the present time because the manufacture of tractors was too heavy for such help. The pickets were members of Local 400, United Automobile Workers, CIO.

A spokesman for the women's committee said that 2,200 men with no seniority had been hired, while 5,000 women wartime workers had not yet been recalled to jobs.

John G. Carney, president of Local 400, said that less than 300 women were employed now, compared with a wartime peak of 5,849.

57

DOROTHY HAENER

Oral History Account on Becoming a Union Activist and Feminist

1978

Before the war Dorothy Haener had worked at low-waged factory jobs. She got hired as a clerk at a Ford Bomber plant in Willow Run, Michigan, and with the help of the UAW got the training necessary to be an inspector. When the war ended, she lost her job and worked in a low-paying toy factory until eventually she was rehired by Ford doing

Dorothy Haener, interviewed by Lyn Goldfarb, Lydia Kleiner, and Christine Miller, 1978, "The Twentieth-Century Trade Union Woman: Vehicle for Social Change," Oral History Project, Institute of Labor and Industrial Relations, University of Michigan, 31–34, 59.

clerical work at substantially less pay than her wartime work. She was
interviewed at age sixty-seven in 1978 by Lyn Goldfarb, Lydia Kleiner,
and Christine Miller. As she explains in this passage from her interview,
her frustration prompted her to become a union activist and eventually
led to her embrace of feminism.

Haener: I really don't think that most women, at least I didn't, believed that we were going to get shafted the way we did, in terms
of employers, you know, using the laws which they had ignored
during the war years, to now say we couldn't work the number
of hours or we couldn't do the weight lifting and all that kind of
thing. . . .

But, in terms of the women, where they did hire the women, primarily, when they started hiring them, was on the sewing machines,
on the jobs that were traditionally considered women's jobs, wom-
en's work. On the small assembly work, they hired women. So that,
you know, there were quite a few of the Local 50 [union] women
who were given jobs because of that hiring. They hired enough of
the Local 50 women under the preferential set-up to say, at least,
"Well, we are hiring them." But myself, you see, my problem was
that I had no history of having been employed at the Ford Bomber
plant, either as an assembler or sewing machine operator. My whole
history was as a clerk or as an inspector. And they were not about to
hire a woman doing inspection.

Interviewer: So they really tried then to get things back the way they
were before the war, they wanted it, to get rid of those changes?

Haener. Yes. . . .

Interviewer: What excuses did they use, because certainly they knew
by that time that women were capable of doing all the work.

Haener: Well, the excuses they would use was that producing airplanes
is different than producing automobiles, that the work on automobiles is much heavier and the women are not going to be able to
do it, and that women really don't want to work in shops with all the
men. And, of course, the other argument is that once they transferred the people from Kaiser-Fraser [which took over from Ford],
there were all these GI's coming back who had to have jobs and
that they ought to be considered and given work. You know, to a
certain extent, they didn't really feel compelled to give any rationale
for it because it was the feeling of people behind the scenes that the

preferential hiring rights agreement [seniority] was not absolutely binding. . . . And, for those reasons, they could go ahead and do pretty much as they pleased. . . .

[In response, Haener got active in the union for the first time and got herself elected to the bargaining committee to put pressure on them to employ women from Local 50 when they were hiring.]

I do remember during that period of time that some of these people were, you know, personal friends of mine who would even call me up at home or come to me and say how desperate they were for a job, which, you know, completely puts to rest this concept that the women didn't want the job. They really desperately wanted the jobs and they knew that if they didn't get a job working at this kind of a plant where wages were good, that they were going to end up the rest of their life like the job I had at the toy factory, you know, that I barely existed on. . . . [W]hen I finally got on the [union] committee, they would come to me and it was just appalling because there was nothing you could do for them until I finally got a couple of the people on the committee [as allies]. . . . I really had to pressure our own people. . . .

And it was a terribly awakening experience for me. . . . And, you know, I really believed all this stuff we preached and believed that everybody was going to do it. And it's a terrible disillusion to you to discover that, having got this far, now really [you] have to fight. . . .

[Her union activism, especially on behalf of women, continued for many decades and led her to be a founding member of the National Organization for Women.]

I don't mind saying either — and I think that most people would agree with you in the UAW who look at it objectively — that speaking out as I have on women's issues has not helped me in the UAW. It's really made life difficult for me in many cases. But it's been worth it to me. I really feel very strongly that if there had not been a few people like us around doing the kinds of things that we have done, that much of what we have seen happen in the Women's Movement might not well have happened. I was among the ten or eleven people who sat in a hotel room with Betty Friedan and put together the concept of NOW.

58

BETTY FRIEDAN

UE Fights for Women Workers

June 1952

Perhaps the most dramatic example of the link between union women's activism and the 1960s feminist movement was the 1952 article extracted below. Written anonymously by Betty Friedan eleven years before her path-breaking book The Feminine Mystique, *the article systematically critiques the discrimination working women face and explicitly condemns the idea of sex-segregated job classifications. Equally interesting, it includes a discussion of the specific problems of black working women and thus hints at the links between women's union activism and civil rights activism in the postwar years. This article has fueled historians' argument that there was a direct connection between the UE women's wartime and postwar efforts to carve out more equal opportunities for blue-collar working women and the feminist movement of the 1960s.*

How Industry Exploits Women Workers

In advertisements across the land, industry glorifies the American woman — in her gleaming GE kitchen, at her Westinghouse laundromat, before her Sylvania television set. Nothing is too good for her — unless she works for GE, or Westinghouse, or Sylvania or thousands of other corporations throughout the U.S.A.

As an employee, regardless of her skill she is rated lower than common labor (male). She is assigned to jobs which, according to government studies, involve greater physical strain and skill than many jobs done by men — *but she is paid less than the underpaid sweeper, the least skilled men in the plant.* She is speeded up until she may faint at her machine, to barely earn her daily bread.

Wage discrimination against women workers exists in every industry where women are employed. It exists because it pays off in billions

United Electrical, Radio and Machine Workers of America, *UE Fights for Women Workers*, UE Publication No. 232, June 1952, 5, 8, 26–27, 37–38.

of dollars in extra profits for the companies. According to the 1950 census, the average wage of women in factories was $1,285 a year less than men. Multiply this by the 4,171,000 women in factories and you get the staggering total of 5.4 billion dollars. In just one year, U.S. corporations made *five billion four hundred million dollars in extra profits* from their exploitation of women. . . .

UE's Battle to End Double Standard

. . . Today, the UE is engaged in an intensified campaign to end the rate discrimination against women. For these rates below common labor threaten every rate in the plant. The companies, as part of their general rate-cutting offensive, are putting in new machines and processes to be run by women at rates below common labor, replacing higher-paid men. And because the women's base rate is so low, they are at the mercy of the company's speed-up drive—the women are being used as a wedge to speed up and cut rates of all workers.

That's why in collective bargaining today, a major UE demand is to abolish all rates below common labor and end the rate discrimination against women. The full weight of the union is being thrown behind this battle. . . .

Special Situation of Negro Women

The situation of Negro women workers today is even more shocking. . . . For the discrimination that keeps Negro men at the bottom of the pay scale forces their wives to work to supplement the pitifully inadequate income of the family.

But Negro women are barred from almost all jobs except low-paying domestic service in private homes, or menial outside jobs as janitresses and scrubwomen. In the basic sections of the electrical, radio and machine industry, as in industry generally, Negro women are not employed. . . .

Census figures show the special economic problems of Negro women:

- 41.4% of Negro married women continue to work compared to 25.3 percent of white married women.
- As of March, 1950, 20.7 percent of Negro women with children under six had to work as compared with 11.2 percent of white women.

- Altogether in 1950, 46 out of every hundred Negro women were in the labor force as compared to 32 out of every hundred white women.

- Out of 451 job classifications, ¾ of all women workers were concentrated in the 23 lowest paid job categories. But almost ⅘ of Negro women workers were employed in 5 of the lowest paid of the 451 job classifications.

- In 1950, the average earnings of Negro women were $474 a year, compared to $1,062 for white women. . . .

UE's fair practices committees in many local unions have been fighting the discrimination against hiring Negro women in the electrical and machine industry, and the discriminatory practices that restrict Negro women to the most menial, lowest-paid jobs. . . . Negro women workers have a real stake in the UE's fight to end rate exploitation of women in the industry, but their problems also require a special fight to lift the double bars against hiring of Negro women. . . .

The Whole Union's Fight

One third of the UE membership are women. If all the women who work in UE plants belonged to the union, the percentage would be even higher. This single fact shows how important for the strength of the union is the fight to end discrimination against women in our plants.

The companies want to keep the women segregated, on separate lower paying jobs with separate seniority, so that they may use them as part of their plan to drive down wages and destroy union gains under their war program. In the layoffs that are resulting from the war economy and the big business runaway shop drive,[1] they want to pit women against men, married women against single workers, older women against younger.

Segregation of women is the handle of a dangerous union-smashing weapon in the hands of the company. The only way to fight it is to end the segregation, integrate the women's jobs in their proper places in the rate structure, make it possible for women to be upgraded to any job in the plant, and establish identical seniority rights based on length of service without regard to age, sex, marital status, race or color.

---

[1]"Shop drive" refers to corporations' efforts to undermine the ability of unions to have a "closed" shop, in which all workers must belong to the union.

Women in the UE are determined to win the rates and job rights to which they are entitled. They have been meeting in conferences all over the country to discuss urgent problems of meeting the high cost of living on paychecks even lower than other workers . . . of physical suffering caused by growing speedup in the plant, coupled with care of home and children after the full workday. They resolved to fight to end the double wage standard that enables the companies to make an extra profit on their sex while they have such a hard time getting along. And these UE women have real fighting power, as they have demonstrated on many a picket line[2] across the country.

[2]Friedan is probably referring to women's participation in a series of UE strikes in 1946, a year characterized by waves of strikes on the part of many unions.

A Chronology of American Working Women
and the World War II Era
(1890–1950)

1890– 1914	Progressive Era.
1914– 1918	World War I.
1914– 1919	First Great Migration of African Americans from the South to the North.
1917– 1918	United States participation in World War I.
	Women workers find expanded opportunities in defense industries that temporarily challenge sex-segregated labor market.
1920	Federal U.S. Women's Bureau created.
1923	Equal Rights Amendment (ERA) introduced in Congress.
1929– 1939	The Great Depression.
1935	Congress of Industrial Organizations (CIO) established.
1939– 1945	World War II.
1940	Second Great Migration of African Americans from the South begins.
1941	Fair Employment Practices Committee (FEPC) created by Executive Order 8802 prohibits racial discrimination in defense industries.
	United States enters World War II.
1942	War Manpower Commission (WMC) and other wartime federal agencies begin operating.
	"Womanpower campaign" to recruit women to defense industries and the military begins.

National War Labor Board decrees that women should be paid equally to men for equal work in defense industries.

Women's Army Auxiliary Corps (WAAC), Naval WAVES, Marine Corps Reserves, and Coast Guard SPARS created by Congress.

Japanese Americans incarcerated in internment camps.

United Automobile, Aircraft and Agricultural Implement Workers of America (UAW) Convention passes resolutions against wage discrimination.

United Electrical, Radio and Machine Workers of America (UE) Convention passes resolution to train more women to serve as union leaders.

1943   Women's Land Army created.

WAAC supplanted by Women's Army Corps (WAC).

Women Airforce Service Pilots (WASP) created.

Rumors about WAACs being issued contraceptives creates scandal.

Federal Works Agency (FWA) assumes federal childcare services.

Thomas Bill to give the U.S. Children's Bureau oversight of federal childcare services fails.

Kaiser shipyards on the West Coast establish childcare centers.

1944   Black WAC unit 6888, led by Charity Adams Earley, is sent to Europe.

Four African American WACs at Fort Devens court-martialed.

Women are 21.8 percent of labor union members.

United Autoworkers Convention passes a resolution calling for extensive efforts to counter discrimination against women workers.

1945   U.S. Women's Bureau reports that 75 percent of defense industry workers wish to keep their jobs, but women workers are laid off at a rate 75 percent higher than men.

UAW women protest layoffs by Ford Motor in Detroit.

U.S. Women's Bureau sponsors conference of union women and creates a Labor Advisory Committee.

1946   Federal childcare centers close.

1946   UAW creates a permanent Women's Bureau.

1950   29 percent of American women are in workforce, compared to 25.4 percent in 1940.

Questions for Consideration

1. This collection offers a wide range of documents, including government reports, magazine and newspaper articles, oral histories, letters, and images. What are the strengths and weaknesses of the different types of material in assessing the experiences of working women in World War II?

2. What assumptions about women workers are evident in the "womanpower" campaign of the War Manpower Commission and the Office of War Information as outlined in Chapter 1 (Documents 1–7)?

3. In what ways do the documents in other chapters support these assumptions? In what ways do they challenge them?

4. What reasons did women give for deciding to work in the defense industry (Documents 8–13, and 14)?

5. Did women's reasons for taking defense jobs or enrolling in the military vary by race or ethnicity (Documents 8–14, 37, 39, and 40)? Explain.

6. What insights do Documents 7, 8, 16–18, 27, 37, 38, and 57 offer concerning African American women's wartime experience? In what ways did they find new opportunities? How did they respond to discrimination?

7. Although there are fewer documents available to us for other women of color, what conclusions can you draw about the experiences of Mexican Americans, Japanese Americans, Chinese Americans, and Native Americans and how they may have differed from the experiences of black and white women (Documents 10–12, 14, 15, 39, 40, and 41)?

8. What problems did women encounter during the second shift (Documents 9, 13, 25, 28–33, and 34)?

9. How did women activists in the United Electrical, Radio and Machine Workers of America and the United Automobile Workers seek to improve women's work lives (Documents 18–27, 56, and 57)? What role did they play in challenging race discrimination (Documents 18, 26, 27, and 58)?

10. What obstacles within the unions did women members encounter (Documents 21, 27, 56, 57, and 58)?

11. Were the reasons for women entering military jobs the same as those who worked in the defense industry (Documents 10, 37, 39, and 40)? Explain.

12. What kinds of work did military women perform (Documents 37–39, 41, 44–46, and 47)?

13. What types of challenges did military women face in terms of public attitudes about competence, sexuality, and respectability (Documents 35–37, 42, and 43)?

14. As the war came to a close, how did public opinion vary on the question of women's continuing participation in the workforce (Documents 48–53, and 55)?

15. What role did labor union women play in the struggle to expand women's work opportunities in the postwar era (Documents 56, 57, and 58)?

16. How would you summarize the short-term and long-term effects of World War II on women's labor?

Selected Bibliography

EARLY TWENTIETH-CENTURY WOMEN'S LABOR

Blackwelder, Julia Kirk. *Now Hiring: The Feminization of Work in the United States, 1900–1995.* College Station: Texas A&M University Press, 1997.

Dumenil, Lynn. *The Second Line of Defense: American Women and World War I.* Chapel Hill: University of North Carolina Press, 2017.

Kessler-Harris, Alice. *Out to Work: A History of Wage-Earning Women in the United States.* New York: Oxford University Press, 2003.

Milkman, Ruth. "Organizing the Sexual Division of Labor: Historical Perspectives on 'Women's Work' and the American Labor Movement." In Ruth Milkman, *On Gender, Labor, and Inequality,* 79–118. Urbana: University of Illinois Press, 2016.

Sealander, Judith. *As Minority Becomes Majority: Federal Reaction to the Phenomenon of Women in the Work Force, 1920–1963.* Westport, Conn.: Greenwood Press, 1983.

Ware, Susan. *Holding Their Own: American Women in the 1930s.* Boston: G. K. Hall and Co., 1982.

Weiner, Lynn Y. *From Working Girl to Working Mother: The Female Labor Force in the United States, 1820–1980.* Chapel Hill: University of North Carolina Press, 1985.

Woloch, Nancy. *A Class by Herself: Protective Laws for Women Workers, 1890s–1990s.* Princeton, N.J.: Princeton University Press, 2015.

WOMEN IN WORLD WAR II

Anderson, Karen. *Wartime Women: Sex Roles, Family Relations, and the Status of Women during World War II.* Westport, Conn.: Greenwood Press, 1981.

Campbell, D'Ann. *Women at War with America: Private Lives in a Patriotic Era.* Cambridge, Mass.: Harvard University Press, 1984.

Faderman, Lillian. *Odd Girls and Twilight Lovers: A History of Lesbian Life in Twentieth-Century America.* New York: Penguin, 1991.

Gluck, Sherna Berger. *Rosie the Riveter Revisited: Women, the War and Social Change.* New York: New American Library, 1987.

Hartmann, Susan M. *American Women in the 1940s: The Home Front and Beyond.* Boston: Twayne, 1982.

Honey, Maureen. *Creating Rosie the Riveter: Class, Gender, and Propaganda during World War II.* Amherst: University of Massachusetts Press, 1984.

Knaff, Dona B. *Beyond Rosie the Riveter: Women of World War II in American Popular Graphic Art.* Lawrence: University Press of Kansas, 2012.

Leder, Jane Mersky. *Thanks for the Memories: Love, Sex, and World War II.* Westport, Conn.: Praeger, 2006.

Litoff, Judy Barrett and David C. Smith, eds. *American Women in a World at War: Contemporary Accounts from World War II.* Wilmington, Del.: Scholarly Resources, 1997.

———, eds. *Since You Went Away: World War II Letters from American Women on the Home Front.* Lawrence: University Press of Kansas, 1991.

May, Elaine Tyler. "Rosie the Riveter Gets Married." In *The War in American Culture: Society and Consciousness during World War II*, ed. Lewis A. Erenberg and Susan E. Hirsch, 128–43. Chicago: University of Chicago Press, 1996.

McEuen, Melissa A. *Making War, Making Women: Femininity and Duty on the American Home Front, 1941–1945.* Athens: University of Georgia Press, 2011.

Rupp, Leila J. *Mobilizing Women for War: German and American Propaganda, 1939–1945.* Princeton, N.J.: Princeton University Press, 1978.

Weatherford, Doris. *American Women and World War II.* New York: Facts on File, 1990.

Westbrook, Robert B. "'I Want a Girl, Just Like the Girl That Married Harry James': American Women and the Problem of Political Obligation." In Westbrook, *Why We Fought: Forging American Obligations in World War II*, 67–92. Washington, D.C.: Smithsonian Books, 2010.

Yellin, Emily. *Our Mothers' War: American Women at Home and at the Home Front during World War II.* New York: Free Press, 2004.

WORKING WOMEN DURING WORLD WAR II

Boris, Eileen Boris. "'You Wouldn't Want One of 'Em Dancing with Your Wife': Racialized Bodies on the Job in World War II." *American Quarterly* 50 (1998): 77–108.

Carpenter, Stephanie A. *On the Farm Front: The Women's Land Army in World War II.* De Kalb: Northern Illinois University Press, 2003.

Gabin, Nancy F. *Feminism in the Labor Movement: Women and the United Auto Workers, 1935–1975.* Ithaca, N.Y.: Cornell University Press, 1990.

Kesselman Amy. *Fleeting Opportunities: Women Shipyard Workers in Portland and Vancouver during World War II and Reconversion.* Albany: State University of New York Press, 1987.

Laughlin, Kathleen A. *Women's Work and Public Policy: A History of the Women's Bureau, U.S. Department of Labor.* Boston: Northeastern University Press, 2000.

Milkman, Ruth. *Gender at Work: The Dynamics of Segregation by Sex during World War II*. Urbana: University of Illinois Press, 1987.

Puaca, Laura Micheletti. *Searching for Scientific Womanpower: Technocratic Feminism and the Politics of National Security, 1940–1980*. Chapel Hill: University of North Carolina Press, 2014.

Riley, Susan E. "Caring for Rosie's Children: Federal Child Care Policies in the World War II Era." *Polity* 26 (Summer 1994): 655–75.

United States Department of Labor Women's Bureau and Mary Elizabeth Pidgeon. *Changes in Women's Occupations, 1940–1950: Women's Bureau Bulletin No. 253*. Washington, D.C.: U.S. Government Printing Office, 1954.

———. *Changes in Women's Employment during the War: Special Bulletin No. 20 of the Women's Bureau*. Washington: D.C.: U.S. Government Printing Office, 1944.

———. *Employment of Women in the Early Postwar Period: Women's Bureau Bulletin, No. 211*. Washington, D.C.: U.S. Government Printing Office, 1946.

Vosko, Leah F., and David Witwer. "'Not a Man's Union': Women Teamsters in the United States during the 1940s and 1950s." *Journal of Women's History* 13 (Autumn 2001): 169–92.

Yesil, Bilge. "'Who Said This Is a Man's War?' Propaganda, Advertising Discourse and the Representation of War Worker Women during the Second World War." *Media History* 10 (2004): 103–17.

WOMEN OF COLOR DURING WORLD WAR II

Anderson, Karen Tucker. "Last Hired, First Fired: Black Women Workers during World War II." *Journal of American History* 69 (June 1982): 82–97.

Chavez, Carmen. "Coming of Age during the War: Reminiscences of an Albuquerque Hispana." *New Mexico Historical Review* 70 (October 1995): 396–97.

Escobedo, Elizabeth R. *From Coveralls to Zoot Suits: The Lives of Mexican American Women on the World War II Homefront*. Chapel Hill: University of North Carolina Press, 2013.

Fehn, Bruce. "African-American Women and the Struggle for Equality in the Meatpacking Industry, 1904–1960." *Journal of Women's History* 10 (Spring 1998): 45–69.

Gouveia, Grace Mary. "'We Also Serve': American Indian Women's Role in World War II." *Michigan Historical Review* 20 (Fall 1994): 153–82.

Honey, Maureen, ed. *Bitter Fruit: African American Women in World War II*. Columbia: University of Missouri Press, 1999.

Kersten, Andrew E. "Jobs and Justice: Detroit, Fair Employment, and Federal Activism during the Second World War." *Michigan Historical Review* 25 (Spring 1999): 76–101.

———. *Race, Jobs, and the War: The FEPC in the Midwest, 1941–46*. Urbana: University of Illinois Press, 2007.

Matsumoto, Valerie. "Japanese American Women during World War II." In *Unequal Sisters: A Multi-Cultural Reader in U.S. Women's History*, ed. Ellen Carol DuBois and Vicki L. Ruiz. New York: Routledge,1990.

Moore, Shirley Ann. *To Place Our Deeds: The African American Community in Richmond, California, 1910–1963*. Berkeley: University of California Press, 2001.

Ruiz, Vicki L. *Cannery Women, Cannery Lives: Mexican Women, Unionization, and the California Food Processing Industry*. Albuquerque: University of New Mexico Press, 1978.

Sánchez, Joanne Rao. "The Latinas of World War II: From Familial Shelter to Expanding Horizons." In *Beyond the Latino World War II Hero: The Social and Political Legacy of a Generation*, ed. Maggie Rivas-Rodríguez and Emilio Zamora, 63–89. Austin: University of Texas Press, 2009.

Santillán, Richard. "Rosita the Riveter: Midwest Mexican American Women during World War II, 1941–1945." *Perspectives in Mexican American Studies* 2 (1989): 132.

Shockley, Megan Taylor. *"We, Too, Are Americans": African American Women in Detroit and Richmond, 1940–1954*. Urbana: University of Illinois Press, 2004.

Turk, Katherine. "'A Fair Chance to Do My Part of Work': Black Women, War Work, and Rights Claims at the Kingsbury Ordnance Plant." *Indiana Magazine of History* 108 (2012): 209–44.

Williams, Rhonda. *Politics of Public Housing: Black Women's Struggles against Urban Inequality*. New York: Oxford University Press, 2004.

MILITARY WOMEN

Berube, Allan. *Coming Out under Fire: The History of Gay Men and Women in World War II*. New York: Free Press, 1990.

Bolzenius, Sandra M. *Glory in Their Spirit: How Four Black Women Took on the Army during World War II*. Urbana: University of Illinois Press, 2018.

Earley, Charity Adams. *One Woman's Army: A Black Officer Remembers the WAC*. College Station: Texas A&M University Press, 1989.

Hampf, M. Michaela. "'Dykes' or 'Whores': Sexuality and the Women's Army Corps in the United States during World War II." *Women's Studies International Forum* 27 (2004): 12–30.

Jackson, Kathi. *They Called Them Angels: American Military Nurses of World War II*. Lincoln: University of Nebraska Press, 2000.

Meyer, Leisa D. *Creating GI Jane: Sexuality and Power in the Women's Army Corps during World War II*. New York: Columbia University Press, 1996.

Monahan, Evelyn M., and Rosemary Neidel-Greenlee. *A Few Good Women: America's Military Women from World War I to the Wars in Iraq and Afghanistan*. New York: Knopf, 2010.

———. *And If I Perish: Frontline U.S. Army Nurses in World War II*. New York: Anchor Books, 2003.

Moore, Brenda L. *Serving Our Country: Japanese American Women in the Military during World War II.* New Brunswick, N.J.: Rutgers University Press, 2003.

———. *To Serve My Country, to Serve My Race: The Story of the Only African-American WACs Stationed Overseas during World War II.* New York: New York University Press, 1996.

Putney, Martha S. *When the Nation Was in Need: Blacks in the Women's Army Corps during World War II.* Metuchen, N.J.: The Scarecrow Press, 1992.

Roberts, Marjorie H. *Wingtip to Wingtip: 8 WASPs, Women's Airforce Service Pilots of World War II.* Aviatrix Publishing, 2000.

Treadwell, Mattie. *The United States Army in World War II, Special Studies, the Women's Army Corps.* Washington, D.C.: Office of the Chief of Military History, 1954.

THE END OF THE WAR AND BEYOND

Cobble, Dorothy Sue. *The Other Women's Movement: Workplace Justice and Social Rights in Modern America.* Princeton, N.J.: Princeton University Press, 2004.

Deslippe, Dennis A. *"Rights, Not Roses": Unions and the Rise of Working-Class Feminism, 1945–80.* Urbana: University of Illinois Press, 2000.

Harrison, Cynthia. *On Account of Sex: The Politics of Women's Issues, 1945–1968.* Berkeley: University of California Press, 1988.

Horowitz, Daniel. *Betty Friedan and the Making of "The Feminine Mystique."* Amherst: University of Massachusetts Press, 2000.

Laughlin, Kathleen A. *Women's Work and Public Policy: A History of the Women's Bureau, U.S. Department of Labor, 1945–1970.* Boston: Northeastern University Press, 2000.

May, Elaine Tyler. *Homeward Bound: American Families in the Cold War Era.* New York: Basic Books, 1988.

Meyerowitz, Joanne, ed. *Not June Cleaver: Women and Gender in Postwar America, 1945–1960.* Philadelphia: Temple University Press, 1994.

Weiss, Jessica. *To Have and To Hold: Marriage, the Baby Boom and Social Change.* Chicago: University of Chicago Press, 2000.

Acknowledgments (continued from page iv)

Document 7: Anna M. Rosenberg, "Womanpower and the War," *Opportunity*, April 1943, pp. 35–36. Reprinted by permission of the National Urban League.

Document 8: Matilda Foster, Oral history transcript / interviews conducted by David Washburn and Tiffany Lok in 2005, BANC MSS 2008/110, © The Regents of the University of California, Oral History Center, The Bancroft Library, University of California, Berkeley. Reprinted by permission.

Document 9: Marian Sousa, Oral history transcript / interviews conducted by Kathryn Stine in 2002, BANC MSS 2008/110, © The Regents of the University of California, Oral History Center, The Bancroft Library, University of California, Berkeley. Reprinted by permission.

Document 10: Maggie Gee, Oral history transcript / interviews conducted by Leah McGarrigle, Robin Li, and Kathryn Stone in 2003, BANC MSS 2008/110, © The Regents of the University of California, Oral History Center, The Bancroft Library, University of California, Berkeley. Reprinted by permission.

Document 11: Margarita Salazar McSweyn, Oral History Account of Work in a Lockheed Plant, 1980. From Sherna Berger Gluck, *Rosie the Riveter Revisited: Women, the War and Social Change* (New York: New American Library, 1987), 85–97. Reprinted by permission of Sherna Berger Gluck.

Document 12: Faith Traversie, Oral history transcript / interviews conducted by Elizabeth Castle in 2005, BANC MSS 2008/110, © The Regents of the University of California, Oral History Center, The Bancroft Library, University of California, Berkeley. Reprinted by permission.

Document 13: Polly Crow, "A Defense Worker's Letters to Her Husband," June 12, 1944 and January 30, 1945. *Since You Went Away: World War II Letters from American Women on the Home Front*, edited by Judy Barrett Litoff and David C. Smith. Copyright © 1991 by Judy Barrett Litoff and David C. Smith. Reproduced with permission of Oxford University Press through PLSclear.

Document 14: "Mother of Seven Builds B-17s; Has Super Attendance Mark," *Long Beach Airview News*, July 13, 1943, p. 11. Reprinted by permission of The Boeing Company.

Document 19: Proceedings of the Seventh Convention of the United Automobile, Aircraft and Agricultural Implement Workers of America (UAW-CIO) (UAW, 1942), pp. 356–361. Reprinted by permission.

Document 20: Proceedings of the Eighth International Convention of the United Electrical, Radio and Machine Workers of America, 1942, 205–206. Reprinted by permission.

Document 21: "Rosie the Riveter Wants Man's Pay, Lady's Respect" *Augusta Chronicle*, December 11, 1944, A-8. Reprinted by permission.

Document 23: "And We Say—," *Ammunition*, Volume 2, No. 9, August 1944, p. 1. Reprinted by permission of United Auto Workers (UAW).

Document 24: "You Have Only One Life to Live," *Ammunition*, Volume 2, No. 9, August 1944, p. 18. Reprinted by permission of United Auto Workers (UAW).

Document 25: "What Do You Care about Children?" *Ammunition*, Volume 2, No. 9, August 1944, p. 26. Reprinted by permission of United Auto Workers (UAW).

Document 26: "Report of UAW-CIO's Women's Conference (Detroit, Dec. 8–9, 1944) to International Executive Board," United Auto Worker War Policy Division, Victor Reuther Collection, Box 2, Folder: "Conferences," Wayne State University. Reprinted by permission.

Document 28: Nell Giles, "Gas Ration Vital to Factory Worker," from *The Boston Globe*, July 29, 1942, p. 15. Copyright © 1945 Boston Globe Media Partners. All rights reserved. Used under license.

Document 31: Marye Stumph, Oral History Account of an Aviation Worker's Solution to Childcare, 1982. From Sherna Berger Gluck, *Rosie the Riveter Revisited: Women, the War and Social Change* (New York: New American Library, 1987), 64. Reprinted by permission of Sherna Berger Gluck.

Document 33: Jane Eads, "Drafting of Fathers Spurs Federal Child Care Program," *Tampa Bay Times*, October 17, 1943, p. 13. Copyright © 1943 Associated Press. Reprinted by permission.

Document 35: "Women of Two Wars," *Saturday Evening Post*, 215 (May 29, 1943). Copyright © SEPS licensed by Curtis Licensing, Indianapolis, IN. All rights reserved. Reprinted by permission.

Document 37: Charity Adams Earley, *One Woman's Army: A Black Officer Remembers the WAC* (College Station: Texas A&M University Press, 1989), pp. 180–81, 186–87. Reprinted by permission of Texas A&M University Press.

Document 38: "Four WACs Sentenced to Hard Labor after Devens Strike," *Baltimore Afro-American,* March 24, 1945, pp. 1 and 2. Reprinted by permission of Afro American Newspapers.

Document 39: Concepción Escobedo, interview by Sandra Freyberg, September 13, 2003, U.S. Latino & Latina World War II Oral History Project, School of Journalism, University of Texas at Austin. Audio tape transcribed by Lynn Dumenil. Reprinted by permission.

Document 40: "Fighting Man's Widow Joins Juarez Squadron," *San Antonio Express*, March 17, 1944, p. 1. Copyright © San Antonio Express-News/ZUMA Press. Reprinted by permission.

Document 44: From *Yes Ma'am!: The Personal Papers of a WAAC Private* by Elizabeth R. Pollack and Ruth F. Duhme. Copyright © 1943 by Elizabeth R. Pollack and Ruth F. Duhme. Reprinted by permission of HarperCollins Publishers.

Document 45: Miriam E. Stehlik Drahos, Letter Describing Service in North Africa, 1943. Pages 81–4 from *With Love Jane: Letters from American Women on the War Fronts* collected and edited by Alma Lutz. Copyright © 1945 by Alma Lutz. Reprinted by permission of HarperCollins Publishers.

Document 46: Anna K. Schelper, Letter Describing Nursing in the Philippines, March 8, 1945. Pages 72–5 from *With Love, Jane: Letters from American Women on the War Fronts* collected and edited by Alma Lutz. Copyright © 1945 by Alma Lutz. Reprinted by permission of HarperCollins Publishers.

Document 47: Interview with Helen Snapp (excerpt), March 14, 2009 (OH.1032), from the collection of The National WW II Museum. All rights reserved. Reprinted by permission.

Document 48: Catherine Hambley, "Asserts Women Be Given Chance in Postwar Era," from *The Washington Post*, March 15, 1945, p. 21. Copyright © 1945 The Washington Post. All rights reserved. Used under license.

Document 49: Marjorie McKenzie, "Pursuit of Democracy," *Pittsburgh Courier*, September 8, 1945, p. 7. Reprinted by permission of the Pittsburgh Courier Archives.

Document 50: Barbara Woollcott, "We Want Our Jobs," from *The Cincinnati Enquirer*, March 4, 1945. Copyright © 1945 Gannett-Community Publishing. All rights reserved. Used under license.

Document 51: Bernice Morgan, "Women War Workers Shun Domesticity; Most of Those Laid Off Hunt New Jobs," from *Rochester Democrat and Chronicle,* August 19, 1945, p. 19. Copyright © 1945 Gannett-Community Publishing. All rights reserved. Used under license.

Document 52: "Most Women Workers Plan to Give Up Jobs after War," *The Seattle Daily Times*, December 25, 1944, II-13. Reprinted by permission of The Seattle Times.

Document 53: Elizabeth Janeway, "Meet a Demobilized Housewife," *Ladies Home Journal,* 62 (November 1945): 158–59, 170. Reprinted by permission of William H. Janeway.

Document 56: "A Complaint from the Women," from *The New York Times*, November 9, 1945, p. 12. Copyright © 1945 The New York Times. All rights reserved. Used under license.

Document 58: United Electrical, Radio and Machine Workers of America, "UE Fights for Women Workers," UE Publication No. 232, June 1952, pp. 5, 8, 26–27, 37–38. Reprinted by permission.

Index